THE TIMES

RYDER CUP

THE ✦ TIMES
RYDER CUP

A complete photographic record from the 1920s to the present day

MATTHEW KNIGHT

First published in 2006 by Times Books, an imprint of HarperCollins*Publishers*
77–85 Fulham Palace Road
London W6 8JB

10 9 8 7 6 5 4 3 2 1
10 09 08 07 06

Images © as follows:
Getty images: pages 3, 6, 7, 8, 9, 12, 14 (both), 15, 16, 18 (both), 19, 20, 21 (top left & bottom), 22 (all), 23 (both), 26, 27, 28, 29 (both), 30 (both), 31 (all), 32, 33, 34, 35, 36 (both), 38, 39, 42, 43, 46, 47 (bottom), 48, 50 (both), 53, 54, 55, 56 (both), 62, 63 (top left & top right), 64, 68, 69 (both), 70 (both), 71 (both), 72, 76, 78, 82 (both), 85, 86 (both), 90, 95, 97 (bottom), 98, 100, 101, 102, 105 (both), 106, 107 (bottom), 108, 109, 110, 111 (both), 112, 113 (all), 114, 115 (all), 116 (both), 117, 118, 119 (both), 120 (both), 121 (both), 122 (both), 123, 124, 125, 126 (both), 127, 128 (both), 129 (both), 130 (both), 131 (both), 132, 133, 134, 135, 136, 137 (both), 138 (both), 139, 140, 141, 142, 143, 144, 145, 146 (both), 147, 148, 149, 151 (top left), 159, 162 (bottom), 165, 166, 169 (bottom), 170 (all), 173, 174, 175 (top right), 177 (bottom), 179 (top right), 183 (both), 184, 187 (top right).
Empics: pages 11, 21 (top right), 37, 40, 41, 44, 46, 47 (top), 49 (both), 51 (both), 57, 58, 59 (both), 63 (bottom), 79, 80, 88, 92 (top right & bottom), 93, 103, 104, 107 (top), 158 (top), 160/161.
Phil Sheldon Golf Photo Library: pages 24/25, 45, 65, 66, 67, 73, 75, 83, 91 (all), 92 (top left), 94, 96 (both), 97 (top).
The Times: pages 150, 151 (top right), 152 (both), 153 (both), 154, 155, 156, 157, 158 (bottom), 160 (bottom right), 161, 162 (top), 163, 164 (both), 167 (both), 168, 169 (top), 171 (both), 172, 175 (top left & bottom), 176, 177 (top), 178, 179 (top left & bottom), 180, 181 (both), 182, 185, 186 (both), 187 (top left), 188, 189.

ISBN 10 - 0 00 724186 0
ISBN 13 - 9 78 0 00 724186 6

British Library Cataloguing in Publication Data
A CIP catalogue record for this book is available from the British Library.

Edited and designed by D & N Publishing
Lambourn Woodlands, Hungerford, Berkshire

Printed in Great Britain by Butler and Tanner, Frome, Somerset

CONTENTS

RYDER CUP

■ 1927–2006 ■

1927 – United States
1929 – Great Britain
1931 – United States
1933 – Great Britain
1935 – United States
1937 – United States

1947 – United States
1949 – United States
1951 – United States
1953 – United States
1955 – United States
1957 – Great Britain
1959 – United States
1961 – United States
1963 – United States
1965 – United States
1967 – United States
1969 – United States (retained)
1971 – United States
1973 – United States
1975 – United States
1977 – United States
1979 – United States
1981 – United States
1983 – United States
1985 – Europe
1987 – Europe
1989 – Europe (retained)
1991 – United States
1993 – United States
1995 – Europe
1997 – Europe
1999 – United States

2002 – Europe
2004 – Europe
2006 – ?

■ *'THIS IS THE FINEST EXPERIENCE IN THE GAME OF GOLF'* ■
Tom Watson – 1993

THE BEGINNING

1921 AND 1926

W HEN THE BRITISH AND AMERICAN GOLFERS ASSEMBLED AT
Gleneagles for the first international professional golf match in
June 1921, the majestic grounds of the Perthshire estate might at
first glance have seemed an appropriate setting for what would evolve into one
of the world's great sporting contests. But a closer inspection revealed a far less
grandiose reality, for the 'Palace of the Glen', much like the Ryder Cup contest
itself, was still under construction and would not be completed for another
three years. The newly opened King's Course, on which the match would take
place, was also a far cry from the meticulously prepared courses of today.
'Rather ragged in appearance,' wrote Bernard Darwin in *The Times*, 'the
bunkers look unkempt and the greens carry more course grass than one likes to
see.' Modern-day professionals would have been horrified at its condition.

Exactly who came up with the idea of staging an international golf match
between the professionals of Great Britain and the United States is the source
of much debate among golf historians. George Sargent, President of the USPGA

Spectators at the 1929 Glasgow Herald
tournament at Gleneagles.

THE BEGINNING

(United States Professional Golfers' Association) from 1921 to 1926, credited the idea to Sylvanus P. Jermain, former President of the Inverness Golf Club in Ohio, whose club hosted the 1920 US Open. That same year, *Golf Illustrated* magazine started a fundraising campaign to send a team from the United States to Britain to play in an international match. This was the brainchild of the magazine's circulation manager, James Harnett, who reasoned that the promotion of such a contest might attract a few more readers. Although Harnett received the enthusiastic support of golfer Walter Hagen, his grand plan came up short of the required funds. It was at this point that the USPGA intervened, and at meeting held on 15 December 1920, the association agreed to provide the rest of the money to fund a trip. With the blessing and financial backing of the USPGA to the tune of $1,000 per player, a first international match was given the go-ahead.

June 1922: 1000 guineas golf tournament at Gleneagles. From left to right, Harry Vardon, Ted Ray, James Braid and J.H. Taylor.

OPPOSITE PAGE

TOP: *'The Haig': Walter Hagen's enthusiasm for international matches was integral to the founding of the Ryder Cup.*

BOTTOM: *Abe Mitchell drives at the first hole at St George's Hill, Weybridge, Surrey, in 1924.*

The next hurdle to overcome was where and when to play the match. A convenient opportunity arose when a professional tournament sponsored by the *Glasgow Herald* was held on the King's Course at Gleneagles on 5 June 1921. With a purse of 1,000 guineas, the event attracted the big names of British golf at that time, notably the great triumvirate of Harry Vardon, James Braid and J.H. Taylor, as well as other top players such as George Duncan, Abe Mitchell, Arthur Havers and Ted Ray. As many of the American players arriving in Britain would be playing not only for the 1,000 guineas but also in the Open Championship being held at nearby St Andrews the following week, it was agreed that an international match would be played the day after the 1,000 guineas tournament.

On 6 June, two weeks after the first unofficial international match for amateurs took place at Hoylake, the professionals of Great Britain and the United States locked horns for the first time. The match was contested over 15 points, with five foursome matches in the morning and ten singles matches in the afternoon. George Duncan captained the British side and Emmett French captained the Americans. While the British were able to field a strong team, the United States weren't blessed with the strength in depth that would become their hallmark once the Ryder Cup started. Apart from Walter Hagen, they were a bit of a mixed bag of home-grown professionals, including Clarence Hackney, Wilfred Reid and William Mehlhorn, and the talented British expatriates Jock Hutchison and Fred McLeod.

Fittingly, the first international foursome match between George Duncan and Abe Mitchell and Walter Hagen and Jock Hutchison was a minor classic. The British pair found themselves two down after four holes, all square after nine, back to two down after 13 and then all square again at the 17th. Mitchell then pulled his ball off the tee on the 18th, but Duncan saved his partner and the match with a recovery shot and then holed a long putt to salvage a half. With another halved match and three wins, Britain finished the morning three points ahead of the United States.

The Americans fared little better in the afternoon, losing a further six singles matches. Hagen did manage another half against Mitchell, and Emmett French beat Ted Ray 2 and 1. But it had been a pretty miserable afternoon for them and they lost heavily 10 ½ points to 4 ½. After the match the teams were presented with commemorative gold medals.

Five years would pass before the next match. Perhaps this was because the Americans thought an international match wasn't such a good idea after all, having been thrashed by Britain, although it's more likely that other players didn't share Hagen's enthusiasm for it. That all changed when Hagen's path crossed with that of Samuel Ryder, who would provide all the help that the American needed.

1921 GLENEAGLES, PERTHSHIRE

GREAT BRITAIN			UNITED STATES
— *FOURSOMES* —			
G. Duncan & A. Mitchell (halved)	½	½	W. Hagen & J. Hutchison (halved)
E. Ray & H. Vardon (5 & 4)	1	0	E. French & T. Kerrigan
J. Braid & J.H. Taylor (halved)	½	½	C. Hackney & F. McLeod (halved)
A.G. Havers & J. Ockendon (6 & 5)	1	0	W. Reid & G. McLean
J. Sherlock & Josh Taylor (1 hole)	1	0	C. Hoffner & W. Mehlhorn
— *SINGLES* —			
G. Duncan (2 & 1)	1	0	J. Hutchison
A. Mitchell (halved)	½	½	W. Hagen (halved)
E. Ray	0	1	E. French (2 & 1)
J.H. Taylor	0	1	F. McLeod (1 hole)
H. Vardon (3 & 1)	1	0	T. Kerrigan
J. Braid (5 & 4)	1	0	C. Hackney
A.G. Havers	0	1	W. Reid (2 & 1)
J. Ockendon (5 & 4)	1	0	G. McLean
J. Sherlock (3 & 2)	1	0	C. Hoffner
J. Taylor (3 & 2)	1	0	W. Mehlhorn
	10½	**4½**	

SAMUEL RYDER AND THE CUP

*In every human being the germ
of golf is implanted at birth, and
suppression causes it to grow and
grow till – it may be at forty, fifty,
sixty – it suddenly bursts its bonds
and sweeps over the victim like
a tidal wave.*

Samuel Ryder.

Many latecomers to golf will attest to the truth of this quote from P.G. Wodehouse's short story 'A Mixed Threesome', and for Samuel Ryder, who discovered the game at the age of 50, the lure of golf proved irresistible. However, few amateur golfers have made such a positive and lasting effect on the game as he.

Samuel Ryder was born in Preston, Lancashire, in 1858, the son of a nurseryman. His first love was cricket, spurred on by the fact that the family lived near the Old Trafford cricket ground. Ryder was just nine when the famous Roses matches between Lancashire and Yorkshire began in 1867, and it's more than likely that he watched many of the competitions. As he grew up he found himself wanting to emulate the Lancashire cricketing legends of the time, Albert Hornby, Alec Watson and the mercurial Johnny Briggs, but his enthusiasm for the sport far outweighed his talent. He joined his father's nursery business and learnt the trade, and it wasn't long before he stumbled across a good idea: selling packets of seeds at a penny each to the general public. Ryder's father didn't share his son's enthusiasm for the idea, however, and it wasn't long before Samuel set out on his own.

In 1895, Sam Ryder moved south to St Albans with his wife and three children and set up a mail-order business selling his penny seed packets. The idea of selling flower and vegetable seeds in small quantities was highly successful, and soon, with the help of his brother James, he founded the Heath and Heather Company Ltd. He soon began to expand the business, marketing and selling herbs.

In his spare time, Ryder was heavily involved in public life. He was a member of the St Albans city council and in 1905 was elected mayor, and he also devoted much of his time and money to the local church. The frenetic pace of Ryder's life most probably caused the breakdown in his health in 1908. His doctor recommended that he should reduce his workload and get some fresh air and exercise, and it wasn't long before someone suggested that Ryder should take up golf. Initially he was reluctant to do so, but he soon became hooked on the game. His practice regime was so intensive – six days a week – that he was able to join the local Verulam Golf Club in 1910 and a year later was appointed captain.

The success of Ryder's seed business was such that it allowed him to start sponsoring professional golf events, and in 1923 the first Heath and Heather tournament took place at Verulam Golf Club. Not only was there a £50 cheque for the winner (a considerable sum for a professional tournament), but it was also the first time professionals received appearance money, with every player guaranteed £5. Naturally, the contests attracted some of the great names of the day, including Harry Vardon, James Braid, J.H. Taylor, George Duncan, Ted Ray and Abe Mitchell. With the first tournament proving to be an overwhelming success for both the business and the professionals, Ryder went on to sponsor a further six events.

It was also during this time that Ryder struck up a friendship with Abe Mitchell. Like many professionals of the day, Mitchell spent most of his time scratching a living as a club professional, in his case at North Foreland Golf Club in Kent. He was a highly talented player and a two-time winner of the British Matchplay Championship, but the biggest prize, the Open Championship, had thus far eluded him. In 1925, Ryder asked Mitchell to become his golf tutor, offering him a handsome salary of £500 per year. With a further £250 allocated to cover the expenses of entering professional events, Ryder hoped his good friend would at last lose the 'best player never to win' tag and take home the Claret Jug.

Ryder's friendship with Mitchell would be the catalyst for the birth of the Ryder Cup matches. With more time to devote to playing professional tournaments and exhibitions, Mitchell would pass on the news from the professional circuit to a rapt Ryder. The Americans, spearheaded by Walter Hagen, were now beginning to dominate the three Major championships, and naturally talk turned to reviving the idea of an international professional

May 1924: Walter Hagen practises his swing on the roof of the Savoy Hotel, London.

match. After all, amateur golfers now had the Walker Cup (established 1922), so why shouldn't the professionals have something similar?

Walter Hagen probably did as much to promote the idea as anyone, and upon hearing that a proposal to stage another match had been formalized, he gladly accepted the responsibility of raising an American team. By 1926, Hagen was at the top of the sport, having established his reputation on both sides of the Atlantic with wins at the 1922 and 1924 Open Championships to go with four other Majors. He was quite simply golf's first superstar. But it wasn't just his great golfing skill that attracted attention. Flamboyant, generous (he once gave his caddie his winner's cheque), cocky and genial, he approached all aspects of life with a rare vigour, best summed up by his phrase 'Don't hurry, don't worry, and stop to smell the roses along the way'. Golf crowds adored him, as did tournament organizers, who craved his presence at their events. His off-course persona would often blur with his feats on course, and he once famously turned up at the 1st tee dressed in his tuxedo, having spent the whole night out on the town.

When Abe Mitchell relayed the news of the proposed international match to Sam Ryder, the old man jumped at the chance to get involved and agreed to provide a cup to mark the event. London silversmiths Mappin and Webb were commissioned to design the solid-gold trophy, adorned with the figure of Abe Mitchell, at a cost of £250.

A date for an international match had become available owing to the oversubscription of the 1926 Open Championship. For the first time in the Open's history, the British PGA (Professional Golfers' Association) decided to hold a series of qualifying events, one of which would held at the Sunningdale Golf Club in Surrey. As many of the American professionals were travelling across the Atlantic to play in the qualifiers, the international match could be staged shortly after them and before the Open itself began. George Duncan, a veteran of the 1921 international, was now the club professional at nearby Wentworth, and so it was decided that the match would be played there on 4–5 June over the recently opened East Course.

On the 4 June 1926, *The Times* reported:

> *The international match between British and American professionals will be begun at Wentworth today, when foursomes over 36 holes will be played. Tomorrow the Singles will be decided, also over 36 holes. The match is for the possession of the 'Ryder' Cup presented by Mr Samuel Ryder*

With Sam Ryder and his daughter Joan among the small crowd, the match got underway. Over two days the teams competed in five 36-hole foursomes and ten 36-hole singles matches. The British team, captained by Ted Ray, boasted a new crop of players – Ernest Whitcombe, Herbert Jolly, Fred Robson, Aubrey

ABOVE: *4 June 1926: Competitors in the International Golf Tournament between Great Britain and America at Wentworth: (l–r) Fred Robson (Britain), Fred McLeod (USA), Ted Ray (Britain) and Cyril Walker (USA).*

RIGHT: *George Duncan of Great Britain tees off at the 4th hole during the unofficial Ryder Cup at Wentworth.*

Boomer, George Gadd and Archie Compston – to add to the more experienced Duncan, Mitchell and Havers. The Americans, led by Walter Hagen, were strengthened by Jim Barnes, Tommy Armour and Jock Stein.

The match itself was a completely one-sided affair – the British professionals beat the Americans by 13½ points to 1½. It's not known what Walter Hagen (partnered by Jim Barnes) thought about being thrashed 9 and 8 by Abe Mitchell and George Duncan in the foursomes, but the score must have embarrassed the great man. He also lost his singles match 6 and 5 to George Duncan, and Abe Mitchell beat Jim Barnes 8 and 7. Only William Mehlhorn and Emmett French claimed any points.

After the match, the players gathered in the clubhouse for champagne and chicken sandwiches and to talk over the matches in what proved to be a convivial atmosphere. It's often thought that the Ryder Cup itself was born out of a conversation held that evening. The story goes that Samuel Ryder said words to the effect of, 'What a wonderful day it has been. We must do this again', which everyone in the room heartily agreed with. At this point, George Duncan is supposed to have turned to Ryder and challenged him to put up a trophy for the event. However, the principle of a Ryder Cup competition had already been established, as the report in *The Times* on the previous day confirms. So why wasn't the cup itself awarded?

By Monday 7 June, the 'Ryder' Cup match had mysteriously changed into the 'International Match' in *The Times* report. The reason for this was that the USPGA didn't sanction the result. Their rules categorically stated that only first-generation citizens could legitimately represent the United States. With a number of British expatriates on the team – Jim Barnes, Tommy Armour, Fred McLeod and Joe Stein – the match and the result were struck from the record books. In addition, Walter Hagen, in what must have been a desperate attempt to make up the numbers, had enlisted the help of his Australian friend, the trick-shot specialist Joe Kirkwood.

Even if the USPGA had been able to sanction the result, it's far from clear whether Sam Ryder had his eponymous cup ready on time anyway. Importantly though, the will to stage a match regularly had been established, and a year later the Ryder Cup would officially begin.

1926 WENTWORTH GOLF CLUB, SURREY

GREAT BRITAIN			UNITED STATES
— *FOURSOMES* —			
A. Mitchell & G. Duncan (9 & 8)	1	0	W. Hagen & J. Barnes
A. Boomer & A. Compston (3 & 2)	1	0	T. Armour & J. Kirkwood
A.G. Havers & G. Gadd (3 & 2)	1	0	W. Mehlhorn & A. Watrous
E. Ray & F. Robson (3 & 2)	1	0	C. Walker & F. McLeod
E.R. Whitcombe & H. Jolly (3 & 2)	1	0	E. French & J. Stein
— *SINGLES* —			
A. Mitchell (8 & 7)	1	0	J. Barnes
G. Duncan (6 & 5)	1	0	W. Hagen
A. Boomer (2 & 1)	1	0	T. Armour
A. Compston	0	1	W. Mehlhorn (1 hole)
G. Gadd (8 & 7)	1	0	J. Kirkwood
E. Ray (6 & 5)	1	0	A. Watrous
F. Robson (5 & 4)	1	0	C. Walker
A.G. Havers (10 & 9)	1	0	F. McLeod
E.R. Whitcombe (halved)	½	½	E. French (halved)
H.J. Jolly (3 & 2)	1	0	J. Stein
	13½	**1½**	

VICTORIOUS CAPTAIN

TED RAY

THE EARLY YEARS

1927–1937

1927

Eleven months after the false start at Wentworth, the first British team members to contest the Ryder Cup were preparing for their historic journey to Worcester Country Club in Boston, Massachusetts. At the beginning of May, three weeks before the players set sail to New York, Samuel Ryder unveiled his gleaming new trophy, adorned with the figurine of Abe Mitchell, at Verulam, his home club. The match had been arranged, the players were set, and this time the cup was ready. But in the months leading up to the team's departure, it wasn't clear whether they would be travelling at all. Ryder had provided the cup and given it in trust to the PGA, but he made no provision for the cost of sending the players over to America. With the PGA unable to fit the bill either, a public appeal was launched in *Golf Illustrated*, asking its readers to donate money towards the £3,000 trip. When the appeal failed to raise the necessary funds, a further plea for finance was made to all British golf clubs, but out of 1,750 clubs contacted, only 216 responded. With the match in real jeopardy, it fell to Sam Ryder and George Philpot, the editor of *Golf Illustrated*, to make up the shortfall.

There were further agonies to endure, as hours before the team departed Abe Mitchell – who was the captain – was struck down with appendicitis and would have to stay at home. In Mitchell's absence it was agreed that 50-year-old Ted Ray would fill the breach. The players that eventually stepped on to the SS *Aquitania* at Southampton docks were Ted Ray, George Duncan, Arthur Havers, Fred Robson, Archie Compston, Herbert Jolly, Aubrey Boomer and Charles Whitcombe. Along with Mitchell there would be another notable absentee: Samuel Ryder's health had persisted in troubling him, and it was with regret that he stayed at home.

After a rough Atlantic crossing, the players stepped off the boat in New York to be greeted by the American captain, Walter Hagen, and a host of dignitaries. Rather ill after the voyage and somewhat overwhelmed by the size of the reception, the players were taken off to the Westchester-Biltmore Country Club for a gala dinner to mark their arrival. A long night was followed the next day by a trip to Yankee Stadium to watch Babe Ruth's New York Yankees play the

Washington Senators. Still thoroughly exhausted from the journey, the players declined Hagen's offer of a night on the town and staggered back to their hotels for a good night's sleep before taking the train up to the Worcester Club the next morning. Upon arrival there they would face an American team led by Walter

RIGHT: *Waterloo Station: the GB team start their journey to the Worcester Country Club, Massachusetts.*

BELOW: *21 May 1927: the British Ryder Cup team on the Cunard Liner* Aquitania, *on their way to America. Second from the left is Samuel Ryder.*

Hagen and including Gene Sarazen, Johnny Farrell, Joe Turnesa, Al Watrous, William Mehlhorn, Johnny Golden and Leo Diegel.

On the morning of 3 June 1927, the first official Ryder Cup got underway. The competition's format – which would remain in place until 1959 – was for four 36-hole foursome matches on the first day and eight 36-hole singles matches on the second, with a total of 12 points to be won. All games would be matchplay. Walter Hagen and Johnny Golden played Ted Ray and Fred Robson in the first match. Fittingly, it was a close game, with the American pair coming back strongly after a break for lunch to win the first point in Ryder Cup history at the 35th hole. Britain managed only one point from the three remaining foursome matches, which made the score 3–1 at the end of the first day.

The singles matches turned out to be as one-sided as they had been at Wentworth a year earlier, except this time it was the Americans who annihilated the British, winning all but two of the matches. Ted Ray lost to Leo Diegel 7 and 5, and Abe Mitchell's replacement, Herbert Jolly, crashed to an 8 and 7 defeat against Johnny Golden. After playing indifferently on the first day, George Duncan won his match against Joe Turnesa by holing a birdie putt on the last hole, making the final result USA 9½, Great Britain 2½.

It was officially a rout. 'It was the putting that did it', *The Times* golf correspondent Bernard Darwin explained. 'The British team played well enough through the green, but on the putting greens there was a marked inferiority about the visiting team.' Not that Walter Hagen minded as he gladly accepted the trophy.

1927 WORCESTER COUNTRY CLUB, WORCESTER, MASSACHUSETTS

GREAT BRITAIN			UNITED STATES
— FOURSOMES —			
E. Ray & F. Robson	0	1	W. Hagen & J. Golden (2 & 1)
G. Duncan & A. Compston	0	1	J. Farrell & J. Turnesa (8 & 6)
A.G. Havers & H.C. Jolly	0	1	G. Sarazen & A. Watrous (3 & 2)
A. Boomer & C.A. Whitcombe (7 & 5)	1	0	L. Diegel & W. Mehlhorn
— SINGLES —			
A. Compston	0	1	W. Mehlhorn (1 hole)
A. Boomer	0	1	J. Farrell (5 & 4)
H.C. Jolly	0	1	J. Golden (8 & 7)
E. Ray	0	1	L. Diegel (7 & 5)
C.A. Whitcombe (halved)	½	½	G. Sarazen (halved)
A.G. Havers	0	1	W. Hagen (2 & 1)
F. Robson	0	1	A. Watrous (3 & 2)
G. Duncan (1 hole)	1	0	J. Turnesa
	2½	**9½**	

VICTORIOUS CAPTAIN

WALTER HAGEN

1929

The build-up to the second Ryder Cup match at Moortown Golf Club near Leeds was marred by the typically unpredictable British weather. Rain lashed down, helped on by easterly winds, as the players did their best to practise before the competition started.

Still captained by Walter Hagen, the American team had arrived with seven of the players who had won in 1927. Al Espinosa, Ed Dudley and Horton Smith all made their debuts. After their crushing defeat at the Worcester Club the British had decided to bring in some talented youngsters, led by 22-year-old Henry Cotton. Charles Whitcombe's brother Ernest also joined the team, as did Stewart Burns. George Duncan was made captain and, much to the delight of Sam Ryder, Abe Mitchell returned, minus his appendix.

United States captain Walter Hagen hands J.H. Batley, Chairman of the Golfers Association, the Ryder Cup on arrival at Paddington, London.

ABOVE: *Walter Hagen points out various landmarks to his Ryder Cup team-mates on the roof of the Savoy Hotel, London.*

BELOW: *Moortown Golf Club, Leeds 1929: (l–r) Walter Hagen, Samuel Ryder and George Duncan at the pre-match banquet.*

ABOVE: *Members of the second GB Ryder Cup team: (back row, l–r) Henry Cotton, Fred Robson, Archie Compston, Ernest Whitcombe and Stewart Burns; (front row, l–r) Aubrey Boomer, Abe Mitchell, George Duncan (Capt.) and Charles Whitcombe.*

ABOVE: *26 April 1929: Moortown Golf Club, Leeds – the two captains, George Duncan and Walter Hagen.*

BELOW: *Leo Diegel drives at the 18th during his match with Abe Mitchell. Diegel thrashed the Briton 8 and 6 in the singles.*

By the first day of the competition the rain had blown away, and a massive crowd of 10,000 spectators turned up to watch. Much of their attention was focused on the opening match between Charles Whitcombe and Archie Compston and Johnny Farrell and Jim Turnesa. It turned into a close battle, with the Americans one up after 18 holes. But as the British pair fought back – at one stage they were two up – the crowd became increasingly excitable, cheering away at just about anything. Bernard Darwin was not amused:

> *It was a crowd that did not, I imagine, know a great deal about golf. While realizing that golf does not give so many opportunities of shouting as football, they were resolved to make the difference between the two games as small as possible. So they ran, cheered and once, I'm afraid to say, forgot themselves so far as to cheer when an American missed a short putt.*

Still, they couldn't get Whitcombe and Compston over the finishing line and the British pair had to settle for a half. After Espinosa and Diegel beat Duncan and Boomer 7 and 5, and Hagen and Golden beat Cotton and Ernest Whitcombe by two holes, the Americans finished the day leading by 2½–1½.

The second day saw a resurgent Britain fight back. Charles Whitcombe played beautifully to trounce Johnny Farrell 8 and 6, and George Duncan went two better, recording another win over Walter Hagen and beating him 10 and 8. This gave Britain the lead and the momentum it needed. With Compston and Boomer securing comfortable victories over Sarazen and Turnesa, the team was just one point away from winning. All that remained to be decided was who would have the honour of claiming the point that won the Cup.

For a long time it looked as though Ernest Whitcombe, who was two up on the 15th tee against Al Espinosa, would claim the overall win. But Henry Cotton, who

had been all square at lunch with Al Watrous, surged into a three-hole lead in the afternoon. Not for the last time in his career, Cotton stole the show. As Whitcombe was lining up a 4ft putt on the 16th green to go two up, he heard an almighty cheer from the 15th green. Cotton had won against Watrous 4 and 3, and so had beaten Whitcombe to the Cup point. The spectators, who were beside themselves with joy, cheered Cotton all the way back to the clubhouse. The final score was Great Britain 7, USA 5. If the crowds hadn't put off the Americans, the weather most certainly did, the rain and wind returning to disrupt their rhythmic swings.

ABOVE LEFT: *Gene Sarazen tees off at the 18th at Moortown Golf Club, Leeds, during the second Ryder Cup.*

ABOVE: *Samuel Ryder presents George Duncan with the trophy after Great Britain defeated the United States 7–5.*

1929 MOORTOWN GOLF CLUB, LEEDS

GREAT BRITAIN			UNITED STATES
— FOURSOMES —			
C.A. Whitcombe & A. Compston (halved)	½	½	J. Farrell & J. Turnesa (halved)
A. Boomer & G. Duncan	0	1	L. Diegel & A. Espinosa (7 & 5)
A. Mitchell & F. Robson (2 & 1)	1	0	G. Sarazen & E. Dudley
E.R. Whitcombe & T.H. Cotton	0	1	J. Golden & W. Hagen (2 holes)
— SINGLES —			
C.A. Whitcombe (8 & 6)	1	0	J. Farrell
G. Duncan (10 & 8)	1	0	W. Hagen
A. Mitchell	0	1	L. Diegel (8 & 6)
A. Compston (6 & 4)	1	0	G. Sarazen
A. Boomer (4 & 3)	1	0	J. Turnesa
F. Robson	0	1	H. Smith (4 & 2)
T.H. Cotton (4 & 3)	1	0	A. Watrous
E.R. Whitcombe (halved)	½	½	A. Espinosa (halved)

VICTORIOUS CAPTAIN

GEORGE DUNCAN

7   5

1931

The thorny issue of eligibility, which had rendered the first match at Wentworth void, would reappear in 1931, although this time it was the British who faced problems. Three young talented professionals – Percy Alliss (father of Peter), Aubrey Boomer and Henry Cotton – were all expected to make the trip to the Scioto Country Club in Ohio to face the United States team. But the selection rules agreed by both the PGA and USPGA required that the professionals were not only natives but were also resident in the country at the time of selection. This immediately ruled out Alliss and Boomer, as they were working as club professionals in Berlin and Paris respectively. Henry Cotton, meanwhile, was living in Britain but after playing the Ryder Cup planned to stay on in the United States to compete in more tournaments. The rules stated that players would be eligible to play only if, on completion of the matches, they returned home immediately – the clause was inserted at the behest of the Americans to stop expatriot British professionals who were living and working in America (of which there were many) from representing Britain. The rule interfered with Cotton's plans and he declined the invitation to play. He was also unhappy about abiding by the team rule stipulating that any money made from exhibition matches during the team's stay in the United States would be split equally between the players.

Although Cotton was viewed as difficult and, in some eyes, unpatriotic, the PGA was still desperate to have him on the team and urged him to rethink his position. But Cotton was having none of it and went public, writing a letter to *Golf Illustrated* explaining his point of view. The PGA was incensed but still offered him a place on condition that he made a full apology for causing such a ruckus. This was anathema to the free-spirited Cotton, and he refused to play.

The upshot of all this was that Britain took a weakened side to the United States.

OPPOSITE PAGE

26 June 1931: Spectators crowd around the 18th green at Scioto Country Club, Ohio, as George Duncan of Great Britain putts.

Bert Hodson, W.H. Davies and Syd Easterbrook joined Cup stalwarts Mitchell, Compston, Duncan, the Whitcombe brothers, Robson and Havers.

While the British PGA and Henry Cotton were squabbling, the USPGA organized a qualifying tournament for the remaining places on the American team. Hagen, Sarazen, Farrell, Espinosa and Diegel had been picked by the selection committee, but the remaining four players would be chosen from a group of 13 who would undergo a gruelling 90-hole qualifier at Scioto in the week leading up to the competition itself. The top four players in the qualifier – Billy Burke, Wiffy Cox, Craig Wood and Denny Shute – all made the team.

The searing 100°F heat at Scioto Country Club in Ohio could not have been more different from the freezing temperatures at Moortown in Yorkshire. If the Americans hadn't adjusted to the cold at Moortown, then the British were about to find the heat of an Ohio summer equally debilitating.

The pairing of Gene Sarazen and Johnny Farrell overwhelmed Archie Compston and W.H. Davies 8 and 7, and Walter Hagen and Denny Shute saw off Duncan and Havers after just 27 holes. Abe Mitchell and Fred Robson claimed the only British point of the day, with a close 3 and 1 win over Leo Diegel and Al Espinosa. But when Billy Burke and Wiffy Cox closed out Syd Easterbrook and Ernest Whitcombe, the United States had established a 3–1 lead going into the singles matches the next day.

The singles provided no respite from the weather or the Americans, as Compston, Robson and Hodson all suffered massive defeats. In the course of beating Fred Robson 7 and 6, Gene Sarazen played what he rated as his greatest shot ever – even better than his albatross at the 15th at the Masters in 1935. A wild drive at the par-three 4th had sent Sarazen's ball fizzing into a storm shelter at the back of the green. Upon finding his ball, he reasoned that he could play it as it lay. He scooped the ball up with a wedge from the concrete floor, sending it through the open window and onto the green.

Similarly impudent was Walter Hagen's pre-match warm-up. When Charles Whitcombe arrived at the 1st tee he found Hagen coolly sipping a martini from a cocktail glass. When the starter called Hagen's name, he downed the martini and then hit a spanking drive down the middle of the fairway – Whitcombe lost 4 and 3. Although W.H. Davies and Arthur Havers both pulled off 4 and 3 wins against Johnny Farrell and Craig Wood respectively, Britain had simply been outplayed.

1931 SCIOTO COUNTRY CLUB, COLUMBUS, OHIO

GREAT BRITAIN			UNITED STATES
— FOURSOMES —			
A. Compston & W.H. Davies	0	1	G. Sarazen & J. Farrell (8 & 7)
G. Duncan & A.G. Havers	0	1	W. Hagen & D. Shute (10 & 9)
A. Mitchell & F. Robson (3 & 1)	1	0	L. Diegel & A. Espinosa
S. Easterbrook & E.R. Whitcombe	0	1	W. Burke & W. Cox (3 & 2)
— SINGLES —			
A. Compston	0	1	W. Burke (7 & 6)
F. Robson	0	1	G. Sarazen (7 & 6)
W.H. Davies (4 & 3)	1	0	J. Farrell
A. Mitchell	0	1	W. Cox (3 & 1)
C.A. Whitcombe	0	1	W. Hagen (4 & 3)
B. Hodson	0	1	D. Shute (8 & 6)
E.R. Whitcombe	0	1	A. Espinosa (2 & 1)
A.G. Havers (4 & 3)	1	0	C. Wood

VICTORIOUS CAPTAIN

WALTER HAGEN

3   9

1933

After Britain's dismal showing at Scioto, the British PGA turned to J.H. Taylor, five times Open Champion and member of the great triumvirate that included Harry Vardon and James Braid, to captain the team. It was the first time that Britain had selected a non-playing captain, but Taylor, a renowned disciplinarian (he'd initially pursued a military career), would play a far from passive role. Unhindered by the controversy surrounding the selection of Henry Cotton (now employed by the Royal Waterloo Golf Club in Belgium), Taylor set about choosing the strongest team available. Mitchell, Havers, Davies, Easterbrook and Charles Whitcombe all returned for duty, and Alliss, Padgham, Perry and Lacey were drafted in to face the American team. For their part the Americans returned six players from Scioto – Hagen, Sarazen, Shute, Wood, Diegel and Burke – who were accompanied by debutants Paul Runyan, Olin Dutra and Ed Dudley.

Gene Sarazen and Walter Hagen. By June 1933 Hagen had won all 11 of his major championships. Sarazen had collected five, and would win the USPGA Championship later that year.

Taylor wasted no time in getting his boys into shape. As they had wilted in the heat two years earlier, he wasn't going to take any chances and imposed a strict fitness regime – they were woken at 6am and sent running along Southport beach to improve their stamina. The Americans took things a bit easier, with Walter Hagen suggesting they go out on the town instead – true to form, they ended up getting involved in a dance contest!

Taylor's old school discipline and Hagen's 'don't hurry, don't worry' approach was never going to mix and was bound to cause friction at some point. And so it did. When it came to handing over the team-sheets at the 1st tee on the first morning, Hagen failed to show up twice and Taylor threatened to call off the match.

When the match did get underway it turned into a classic. With the prospect of a close match and a royal attendee, the Prince of Wales, the crowds swelled to 15,000. It was quite an occasion, as Bernard Darwin noted in *The Times*: 'There were flags waving everywhere and tents full of sandwiches and beer and golfing sideshows in the nature of a funfair. A gentleman with a megaphone announced the players on the teeing ground in the manner of a master of the ceremonies at a village concert. Thus, "Mr Sarazen will now drive the first ball for America."'

The Prince of Wales, later Edward VIII (1894–1972), watching the progress of the Runyan and Alliss match during the Ryder Cup at Southport. Alliss won 2 and 1.

The foursomes provided wonderful entertainment for the crowd, with three of the matches going the distance. The British were up in all the matches at the halfway point, but Alliss and Whitcombe let slip a three-hole advantage and eventually halved with Sarazen and Hagen. Mitchell and Havers beat Dutra and Shute 3 and 2, and with the last two points shared, Britain won the foursomes by one point.

On the second day, and with four points needed to claim victory, the British challenge got off to a mixed start. Gene Sarazen comfortably beat Alf Padgham 6 and 4, but Mitchell outclassed Dutra, beating him 9 and 8. Hagen brought the scores level with a 2 and 1 win over Lacey, and the match looked set for a tight finish. Apart from Havers beating Diegel 4 and 3, the final four matches were horribly tense, the news of which drew even more crowds through the gates.

Percy Alliss, who'd been one up against Runyan at lunch but whose lead had slipped during the afternoon, found himself all square at the 15th. After Alliss regained the lead at the 16th, the nerves got to Runyan, and on the next hole he fired his ball out of bounds to hand Alliss a 2 and 1 victory. Horton Smith then repelled a marvellous comeback from Whitcombe, who had been five down at lunch, to claim victory at the 17th.

The match was now tied at 5½ points each, with Easterbrook and Shute left to finish. Both players were on the final green in three after their tee shots found a bunker. As the crowds jostled for position around the green, Walter Hagen stood in the relative calm of the clubhouse surveying the scene and wondered whether he should go and remind Shute of the importance of his putt. But with the Prince of Wales standing next to him, he let the moment pass. 'I knew it would be discourteous to walk out on the future King of England just

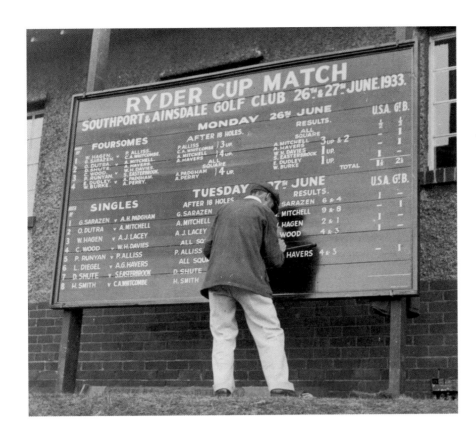

Mid-afternoon and the match is finely balanced, the score tied at 4½ points each.

to whisper in Denny's ear and tell him how to putt', Hagen remarked later. But if only he had. Easterbrook putted up safely and tapped the ball in for a five. Shute, however, raced his ball 4ft past the hole and then missed the return, handing a 6½–5½ victory to Britain.

Accepting the trophy from the Prince of Wales, J.H. Taylor said he was 'the proudest man in all the Commonwealth'. It had been a landmark year for the Ryder Cup. In six short years it had come of age, with record crowds, royal

Walter Hagen tees off at the 2nd during the match at Southport.

27 June 1933: Britain's Syd Easterbrook and American Denny Shute on the last green at Southport during their epic singles match.

patronage and a classic match. For Sam Ryder it was a proud moment, as he had watched his idea finally blossom into a major sporting occasion. However, his health was slowly deteriorating and it would be the last match he would attend. It was farewell also to Abe Mitchell, who at 46 years old would not represent Britain in the Ryder Cup again.

1933 SOUTHPORT & AINSDALE GOLF CLUB, SOUTHPORT, MERSEYSIDE

GREAT BRITAIN			UNITED STATES
— FOURSOMES —			
P. Alliss & C.A. Whitcombe (halved)	½	½	G. Sarazen & W. Hagen (halved)
A. Mitchell & A.G. Havers (3 & 2)	1	0	O. Dutra & D. Shute
W.H. Davies & S. Easterbrook (1 hole)	1	0	C. Wood & P. Runyan
A.H. Padgham & A. Perry	0	1	E. Dudley & W. Burke (1 hole)
— SINGLES —			
A.H. Padgham	0	1	G. Sarazen (6 & 4)
A. Mitchell (9 & 8)	1	0	O. Dutra
A.J. Lacey	0	1	W. Hagen (2 & 1)
W.H. Davies	0	1	C. Wood (4 & 3)
P. Alliss (2 & 1)	1	0	P. Runyan
A.G. Havers (4 & 3)	1	0	L. Diegel
S. Easterbrook (1 hole)	1	0	D. Shute
C.A. Whitcombe	0	1	H. Smith (2 & 1)
	6½	**5½**	

VICTORIOUS CAPTAIN
J. H. TAYLOR (in 1922)

1935

The win at Southport gave rise to genuine hope that Britain, after two comprehensive defeats on American soil, could at last mount a significant challenge. The British PGA was so confident of this that it even took out insurance on the trophy for the return journey from Ridgewood Country Club in New Jersey. 'I feel no team could go to America with a greater opportunity of success than Whitcombe and the boys', declared the confident PGA Secretary Commander R.T.C. Roe. Further belief came when the Americans agreed to delay the start of the contest until September, so as to avoid the oppressive summer heat.

   Charles Whitcombe would captain the side for a second time and would be joined by his two brothers, Ernest, and, for the first time, Reg. Along with newly crowned Open Champion Alf Perry and some of the Southport heroes, Whitcombe also had the services of four talented rookies: Dick Burton, Jack Busson, Ted Jarman and Bill Cox.

   Walter Hagen, in his last Ryder Cup match as a player, also called up four rookies: Johnny Revolta, Henry Picard, Sam Parks and Ky Laffoon. In addition, Dutra, Sarazen, Runyan, Smith and Wood all returned.

   The British confidence ahead of the match took a severe dent on the first day, in what would be the most one-sided set of foursome matches since the tournament had begun. Perry and Busson, Padgham and Alliss, and Cox and

TOP: *The British Ryder Cup team at Leatherhead, Surrey: (l–r) Charles Whitcombe, Alf Padgham, Ernest Whitcombe, Bill Cox, Reg Whitcombe, Jack Busson, Ted Jarman, Percy Alliss, Commander Rowe and Alf Perry.*

ABOVE: *Golfing brothers Ernest, Reg and Charles Whitcombe, the only time three brothers have appeared in the Ryder Cup.*

Jarman were all heavily defeated. Only Charles and Ernest Whitcombe won their match, and this by just one hole.

By mid-afternoon on the second day, Britain had surrendered the Cup. Four straight American wins had left the team with the task of restoring some pride. Percy Alliss came back from three behind at lunch, and recorded the narrowest of victories with a one-hole win over Craig Wood, but all had been disastrously lost. With the competition effectively over, attention turned to the final singles match, where a private battle between the reigning US Open and British Open champions, Sam Parks and Alf Perry, was developing into a classic. Perry went into the 36th hole one up and was favourite to win, right down to the penultimate putt. With his ball lying just inches from the hole, Perry had assured his par four. The American was 40ft away in two, with only an outside chance of a birdie. To everyone's astonishment he holed the putt, squared the match and provided a fitting end to the day's proceedings.

Overall, the Britons had played poorly. Set against the expectations that were drummed up prior to the match, it was inevitable that they received a public dressing-down in the newspapers. It was, said Bernard Darwin, 'yet another American tragedy'. Others weren't quite so reserved. *Golf Illustrated* said the team had 'played about as badly as it knew how', and *Time* magazine followed its headline 'Ryder Rout' by saying that the British had been 'roundly whipped, in a tournament distinguished more by the US team's off-the-course uniforms than by the quality of anyone's game'.

1935 RIDGEWOOD COUNTRY CLUB, RIDGEWOOD, NEW JERSEY

GREAT BRITAIN			UNITED STATES
— FOURSOMES —			
A. Perry & J. Busson	0	1	G. Sarazen & W. Hagen (7 & 6)
A.H. Padgham & P. Alliss	0	1	H. Picard & J. Revolta (6 & 5)
W.J. Cox & E.W. Jarman	0	1	P. Runyan & H. Smith (9 & 8)
C.A. Whitcombe & E.R. Whitcombe (1 hole)	1	0	O. Dutra & K. Laffoon
— SINGLES —			
J. Busson	0	1	G. Sarazen (3 & 2)
R. Burton	0	1	P. Runyan (5 & 3)
R. Whitcombe	0	1	J. Revolta (2 & 1)
A.H. Padgham	0	1	O. Dutra (4 & 2)
P. Alliss (1 hole)	1	0	C. Wood
W.J. Cox (halved)	½	½	H. Smith (halved)
E.R. Whitcombe	0	1	H. Picard (3 & 2)
A. Perry (halved)	½	½	S. Parks (halved)

VICTORIOUS CAPTAIN
WALTER HAGEN (in 1933)

3   9

1937

With the death of Sam Ryder on 2 January 1936, buried with his beloved mashie, the Cup lost its founder and professional golfers throughout the world their champion. However, his legacy was by now assured. Eighteen months later, the tournament would witness the final official contribution of perhaps its biggest cheerleader, as Walter Hagen captained the United States team for a sixth and final time.

30 June 1937: Dai Rees putting on the 18th green during the match at Southport.

For all the criticism levelled at the British team for the poor result at Ridgewood, the confidence levels of both the press and players were surprisingly high. Perhaps it was the return to Southport that clouded people's judgement, or an unerring sense that, as all the other previous matches had been won by the home team, Britain would be impervious. But the truth was that America had been getting ever closer to an away victory, with the score 7–5 at Moortown and then 6½–5½ at Southport four years later.

Byron Nelson playing in his first Ryder Cup at Southport. Nelson won the US Masters, his first major, in Spring 1937.

The return of Henry Cotton to the British side inevitably lifted home spirits. During his eight years of exile from the Cup he had won the Open Championship twice, establishing himself as the greatest British player of his generation. His final round of 71 at Carnoustie in 1937, in lashing rain and against a field that included five of America's Ryder Cup team, is considered one of his finest achievements.

Charles Whitcombe would lead the British team for a third time, recalling Perry, Padgham, Cox, Alliss and Burton from Ridgewood. Along with Cotton, Arthur Lacey came back into the side, and two names of the future made their debuts: Sam King and Dai Rees.

On the American team Hagen assumed a non-playing captain's role, so only three players returned from Ridgewood – Sarazen, Revolta and Picard. Denny Shute and Ed Dudley, who had last played at Southport in 1933, also returned, which left space for four rather talented rookies – Sam Snead, Tony Manero, Ralph Guldahl and Byron Nelson. It was a formidable team.

Cotton led out the foursome matches with Padgham against Dudley and Nelson. The Britons expected to win this match and at lunch they were all square.

But, as Bernard Darwin would lament, 'Theirs was indeed a melancholy business' in the afternoon, the pair going down 4 and 2. Lacey and Cox led their match at the halfway point but lost 2 and 1 in what was a close battle throughout. Whitcombe partnered young Dai Rees and together they managed a half point, but it was Percy Alliss and Dick Burton who gained some real ground. They hung on to a two-hole lead from the 29th to the 35th, where they won 2 and 1. The score of 2½–1½ to the Americans was not a disaster yet, but Britain needed to start quickly in the singles in order to stand a chance.

Padgham opened the singles matches against Guldahl. Things started evenly enough, but on the 6th the American holed a huge putt that kickstarted his round.

At lunch, Padgham found himself six down, and two hours later the American had won 8 and 7. Britain then came back with 2½ points. Sam King halved with Denny Shute, while Rees won four holes in a row to go from three down to one up at lunch. He continued his good form in the afternoon, winning 3 and 1. Henry Cotton also had a good day, controlling his match throughout to win 5 and 3. The competition was now tied at 4–4, with four matches still left on the course.

Alliss was involved in another close game, this time against Sarazen, when the American received a lucky break on the par-three 15th. His drive went over the back of the green and landed in the lap of a lady spectator, who jumped up and sent the ball bouncing back on to the green. Sarazen sank the putt to go one up and managed to hold on for the win. When Sam Snead comfortably beat Burton 5 and 4, it looked a hopeless cause. And so it proved, as the final two matches – involving Perry and Lacey – were both lost at the 17th hole. America had recorded a comprehensive and historic victory, winning 8–4.

It was a fitting end to Walter Hagen's Ryder Cup adventure. After collecting the trophy he said, 'I am proud and happy to be captain of the first American team to win on home soil.' The crowd looked on in silent puzzlement, before Hagen added, 'You will forgive me, I am sure, for feeling so at home here.'

Henry Cotton putting on the partly flooded 18th green at Southport. Cotton defeated Tony Manero of the United States 5 and 3 in the singles.

Lord Wardington, chairman of the R and A Championship Committee, presents Walter Hagen with the Ryder Cup.

1937 SOUTHPORT & AINSDALE GOLF CLUB, SOUTHPORT, MERSEYSIDE

GREAT BRITAIN			UNITED STATES
— FOURSOMES —			
A.H. Padgham & T.H. Cotton	0	1	E. Dudley & B. Nelson (4 & 2)
A.J. Lacey & W.J. Cox	0	1	R. Guldahl & T. Manero (2 & 1)
C.A. Whitcombe & D.J. Rees (halved)	½	½	G. Sarazen & D. Shute (halved)
P. Alliss & R. Burton (2 & 1)	1	0	H. Picard & J. Revolta
— SINGLES —			
A.H. Padgham	0	1	R. Guldahl (8 & 7)
S.L. King (halved)	½	½	D. Shute (halved)
D.J. Rees (3 & 1)	1	0	B. Nelson 0
T.H. Cotton (5 & 3)	1	0	T. Manero 0
P. Alliss	0	1	G. Sarazen (1 hole)
R. Burton	0	1	S. Snead (5 & 4)
A. Perry	0	1	E. Dudley (2 & 1)
A.J. Lacey	0	1	H. Picard (2 & 1)
	4	**8**	

VICTORIOUS CAPTAIN
WALTER HAGEN (in 1933)

WORLD WAR II AND THE 1940s

1939–1949

1939–1943

The outbreak of war in Europe in September 1939 put an abrupt halt to preparations for the Ryder Cup. Both Britain and the United States had already selected teams for the match the following November and the Ponte Vedra Country Club in Florida had been chosen as host. Sadly, the club's chance would not come around again, although it still notes 'Selected site for 1939 Ryder Cup' on its scorecard to this day. Walter Hagen had been chosen to captain America for the seventh time, much to the chagrin of Gene Sarazen, who desperately wanted the job, and Henry Cotton was due to captain Britain. For the record, the American team would have been Vic Ghezzi, Ralph Guldhal, Jimmy Hines, Harold McSpaden, Dick Metz, Byron Nelson, Henry Picard, Paul Runyan, Horton Smith and Sam Snead. The British, meanwhile, had selected Jimmy Adams, Dick Burton, Sam King, Alf Padgham, Dai Rees, and Charles and Reg Whitcombe.

With the matches against Britain on hold indefinitely, Walter Hagen and the USPGA came up with the idea of staging a series of Ryder Cup exhibition matches, the proceeds of which would go towards the American Red Cross. The basic format would remain the same, but in the absence of a British team a 'Challenge' team would instead be selected to face the official American team.

The first of these matches was held at Oakland Hills near Detroit in 1940, where the team selected for the 1939 American Ryder Cup took on a Challenge team led by Gene Sarazen that included Ben Hogan, Jimmy Demaret, Tommy Armour and Craig Wood. The Ryder Cup team won 7–5.

Walter Hagen headed a Ryder Cup team for the last time at the 1941 match at the Detroit Golf Club against a Challenge team captained by the great Bobby Jones. Although 39 years old at the time, Jones was still a formidable player and beat Henry Picard 2 and 1 during a surprise 8½–6½ victory for the Challengers. The competition raised an impressive £25,000. Craig Wood took over the captaincy of the official team at Oakland Hills in 1942, and Walter Hagen returned in 1943 to captain the Challengers at Plum Hollow Country Club. Hagen's team lost that match 8½–3½, but by this time the teams were becoming more difficult to raise as the United States had been drawn into the war.

The Duke and Duchess of Windsor greet Walter Hagen, left, during a benefit Red Cross Golf match at Nassau, Bahamas. Hagen teamed with Gene Sarazen against Bobby Jones and Tommy Armour in the 36-hole 'Match of Champions,' which the Duke refereed.

1947

The prospects of a Ryder Cup tournament looked bleak in 1947. The war had left Britain impoverished and the chances that enough money could be raised to send a team to the United States were slim. However, help and money came from an unlikely source, saving the Ryder Cup from extinction.

Robert Hudson was a wealthy businessman from Portland, Oregon, who had successfully sponsored the Portland Open in 1944 and 1945. Much like Sam Ryder, he had found the game late in his life and took great pleasure in organizing events for professionals. He ran a food-processing company and once described himself light-heartedly as a 'prune merchant'. Hudson was a spirited and generous man whose stated aim was 'to treat the players – all the big ones and unknown – as if they were guests in his own home'. In this respect he was not a million miles away from old Sam Ryder. Hudson first heard of the financial problems facing the Ryder Cup at the 1946 PGA Championship (which he was sponsoring) and immediately offered his help. It wasn't long before he had agreed to underwrite the cost of the whole match.

Great Britain's Ryder Cup golf team: (back row l–r) E. Green, A. Lees, S.L. King, Max Faulkner, R.W. Horne and Commander Roe (Manager); (front row l–r) C.H. Ward, Fred Daly, Henry Cotton (Capt.), Dai Rees and James Adams. They are pictured at the Royal Mid-Surrey Golf Course, Richmond.

With the finance settled, the British team could be selected. It had been ten years since the last match and just three players survived from the defeat at Southport: Henry Cotton, Dai Rees and Sam King. Max Faulkner would make the first of five appearances; Fred Daly, Arthur Lees and Jimmy Adams each made the first of four; and Charlie Ward would represent his country on a further two occasions. Eric Green and Reg Horne also made the trip but did not play in a single match.

The United States team was led by Ben Hogan, who had won the Hudson-sponsored PGA Championship a year earlier. Sam Snead and Byron Nelson both returned from the 1937 team, having won a further five Major championships since the last Ryder Cup. Lloyd Mangrum, Ed Harrison, Herman Barron, Ed Oliver, Jimmy Demaret, Herman Keiser and Lew Worsham all debuted.

Henry Cotton competes in the 1947 Ryder Cup at the Portland Golf Club, Portland. Cotton and his Great Britain team suffered their heaviest defeat in Ryder Cup matches, losing 11–1.

Robert Hudson wasn't content with just paying for the British team to travel, and went to New York himself to meet them off the *Queen Mary*. He then threw a party for the players at the Waldorf Astoria, and if that wasn't enough, he accompanied them on the four-day train ride to Portland. The team arrived well watered and well fed, but absolutely exhausted.

The weather in Oregon that autumn had been abysmal and October had seen the heaviest rainfall for 65 years. The ball did not run far on the sodden ground, and so it was felt that the Americans, with their longer hitters, would have an advantage. But Henry Cotton had his eye on another edge the Americans had that might not be quite so legitimate. On the practice days Cotton had watched in confused awe at how the Americans seemed able to impart backspin on the ball. As there was no detectable change in their swings, Cotton thought he smelt a rat and so requested that officials inspect the Americans' clubs to check that they hadn't been scuffed up. But Cotton's suspicions were unfounded, and after a thorough inspection all the clubs were declared legal.

On the night before the first foursomes over an inch of rain fell. The course was so wet that officials made a special rule to allow balls that plugged on the fairway to be lifted without penalty.

Within minutes of play getting underway, the heavens opened once again and before long there were puddles all over the fairways and small ponds were forming in the bunkers. The first two British pairings had a terrible time of it. Cotton and Lees took 54 putts in 27 holes and lost 10 and 9 to Oliver and

Worsham. Daly and Ward didn't fare much better, losing 6 and 5 to Snead and Mangrum. The real disappointment came with Rees and King, who had held on to a slender lead all day, only to see it snatched away from them by Nelson and Barron at the 35th hole. And having been two up at lunch, Adams and Faulkner could only marvel at Hogan and Demaret's play in the afternoon as the Americans clawed back to win by two holes. The day had started with a near wash out and ended with a complete whitewash. Could the Americans do it again in the singles?

The answer to that question was, very nearly. Only Sam King, who played in the final pairing, won a point (for the record, he beat Herman Keiser 4 and 3). There was one close match between Lees and Nelson, which Nelson won 2 and 1, but the rest of the British players found themselves shaking hands with their American opponents anywhere between the 13th and 16th greens. The first complete whitewash in Ryder Cup history was avoided, but only just: the final score was America 11, Britain 1.

The match at Portland was important, if only to see that the Cup kept going after the war. The scale of the American victory wasn't altogether surprising, considering that most of the Americans had played more competitive golf over the last few years than their fellow professionals in Britain, many of whom had been obliged to join the war effort. And there wasn't anything illegal about the Americans' equipment; the players were just better. In the circumstances, Henry Cotton's comments seemed well judged: 'I do not think we can ever win a match in your country… all the same golf is a wonderful game and we all love it.'

1947 PORTLAND GOLF CLUB, PORTLAND, OREGON

GREAT BRITAIN			UNITED STATES
— FOURSOMES —			
T.H. Cotton & A. Lees	0	1	E. Oliver & L. Worsham (10 & 9)
F. Daly & C.H. Ward	0	1	S. Snead & L. Mangrum (6 & 5)
J. Adams & M. Faulkner	0	1	B. Hogan & J. Demaret (2 holes)
D.J. Rees & S.L. King	0	1	B. Nelson & H. Barron (2 & 1)
— SINGLES —			
F. Daly	0	1	E.J. Harrison (5 & 4)
J. Adams	0	1	L. Worsham (3 & 2)
M. Faulkner	0	1	L. Mangrum (6 & 5)
C.H. Ward	0	1	E. Oliver (4 & 3)
A. Lees	0	1	B. Nelson (2 & 1)
T.H. Cotton	0	1	S. Snead (5 & 4)
D.J. Rees	0	1	J. Demaret (3 & 2)
S.L. King (4 & 3)	1	0	H. Keiser
	1	**11**	

VICTORIOUS CAPTAIN
BEN HOGAN (in 1949)

1949

Twelve long years had passed since the last match on British soil, and the war had left the country scarred and impoverished. However, the rescheduling of sporting fixtures since 1945 had fuelled the sense that things were returning to normal. Indeed, in 1949 there was much excitement about the forthcoming Ryder Cup match and the chance to watch the Americans in action again, although the hopes of seeing one of the finest golfers of any generation were dashed early in the year.

Ben Hogan was returning to captain the United States team, but he would not be playing. On 2 February, while travelling home to Fort Worth after finishing second in the Phoenix Open, the car in which he was travelling with his wife was ploughed into by a Greyhound bus that had crossed the central reservation. Hogan suffered multiple injuries, including a broken pelvis, collar-bone and ankle, and nearly died. Amazingly, he was out of action for only 11 months, although his recovery did not come in time for him to play at Ganton Golf Club, Scarborough.

Hogan and his team arrived at Southampton docks after a six-day voyage on the *Queen Elizabeth*. Nine players made the trip: Harrison, Snead, Demaret and Mangrum, who had all kept their places from 1947; and Johnny Palmer, Clayton Heafner, Chick Harbert, Stewart Alexander and Bob Hamilton, who all made their debuts.

Word had spread in the United States that food rationing was still in force in Britain, so the team brought with them a vast crate of provisions, paid for by Ryder Cup saviour Robert Hudson. The sight of 600 steaks, rib-eye beef, hams and innumerable rashers of bacon being unloaded from the boat immediately raised the hackles of the British press. When asked for an explanation, Ben Hogan said, 'We aren't going to eat all those steaks ourselves … we want to do some entertaining and give your British golfers some.' Needless to say, the explanation wasn't swallowed and the Americans endured many negative headlines about their well-stocked larder.

September 1949: Ben Hogan, captain of the United States team. He would have played but for an horrific car accident earlier in the year.

The American Ryder Cup team aboard the SS Queen Elizabeth: *(l–r) Bob Hamilton, Sam Sneed, Chick Harbert, Jimmy Demaret, Ben Hogan, Lloyd Mangrum, Dutch Harrison, Clayton Haefner, Johnny Palmer and Ed Dudley.*

The British team was captained by Charles Whitcombe and fielded seven of the players (Faulkner, Adams, Daly, Rees, Ward, Lees and King) who had lost so heavily at Portland. They were joined by 1939 Open Champion Dick Burton and Ken Bousfield.

As the final practice day came to a close and both teams had familiarized themselves with the course, the two captains handed in their playing orders to the officials. Everything was set for the foursomes to start the next morning. It was at this point that Ben Hogan dropped a bombshell and asked to inspect all the clubs being used by the home team. Charles Whitcombe was completely taken aback, but could have no objections, and so the British clubs were summoned. With Whitcombe, Commander Charles Roe (Secretary of the PGA), John Letters (the club manufacturer) and Ed Dudley (US honorary captain) in attendance, Hogan began to inspect each club one by one. Scrupulously running his fingers over every blade, he picked out clubs from several bags and then all of those belonging to Dick Burton. Bernard Darwin,

Chairman of the Royal and Ancient Golf Club Rules Committee and golf correspondent for *The Times*, was hurriedly called to adjudicate on the matter.

The news of Hogan's request spread quickly, and it wasn't long before newspapers on both sides of the Atlantic were demanding a story. With a serious diplomatic situation brewing, Darwin inspected the clubs and then calmly declared that the markings on them weren't too serious and that 'there is nothing that a little filing will not put right'. Once this ruling had been established and the controversy averted, the clubs were sent back to the Ganton Club professional, Jock Ballantine, who spent half the night filing them in readiness for play the next morning.

The controversy surrounding the clubs didn't seem to affect the British players at all, and to the delight of the large crowds they got off to a bright start. Max Faulkner and Jimmy Adams maintained a narrow lead throughout their match against Ed Harrison and Johnny Palmer, eventually winning 2 and 1 at the 35th hole. More success followed as Fred Daly and Ken Bousfield defeated

Three times US Masters Champion Jimmy Demaret won both his matches comprehensively at Ganton in 1949.

Bob Hamilton and Skip Alexander 4 and 2. With the third match going the way of the American pairing Demaret and Heafner, it was left to Arthur Lees and Dick Burton to beat the formidable pairing of Lloyd Mangrum and Sam Snead by one hole. This win put Britain on unfamiliar territory: the team was 3–1 up after the first day.

The Americans needed a quick start on the second day if they were to have any chance of winning. Ed Harrison duly got the team off to a flyer against Max Faulkner, birdying five of the first six holes. Faulkner never recovered the deficit and eventually lost 8 and 7 early on in the afternoon. The second match went the way of the British, as Adams saw off a resilient Johnny Palmer 2 and 1. In the third match, Charlie Ward was level with Sam Snead going in to lunch (both men had scored 68s), but Snead continued his good form in the afternoon while Ward faltered, allowing the American to cruise to an easy 6 and 5 victory.

Their two resounding victories gave the Americans the momentum they needed, and with the comeback in full flow they recorded resounding wins in the last four matches to overtake Britain and retain the trophy. Dai Rees was the exception, beating Bob Hamilton 6 and 4, but the Americans had proved unstoppable. It was one of the great comebacks, and as Bernard Darwin noted in *The Times*, 'The Americans were quite definitely superior, whether in skill or lasting power, and their putting, so uniformly smooth, solid, and consistent, was as near as might be invincible.' The Ryder Cup set sail across the Atlantic once again.

1949 GANTON GOLF CLUB, SCARBOROUGH, NORTH YORKSHIRE

GREAT BRITAIN			UNITED STATES
— *FOURSOMES* —			
M. Faulkner & J. Adams (2 & 1)	1	0	E.J. Harrison & J. Palmer
F. Daly & K. Bousfield (4 & 2)	1	0	R. Hamilton & S. Alexander
C.H. Ward & S.L. King	0	1	J. Demaret & C. Heafner (4 & 3)
R. Burton & A. Lees (1 hole)	1	0	S. Snead & L. Mangrum
— *SINGLES* —			
M. Faulkner	0	1	E.J. Harrison (8 & 7)
J. Adams (2 & 1)	1	0	J. Palmer
C.H. Ward	0	1	S. Snead (6 & 5)
D.J. Rees (6 & 4)	1	0	R. Hamilton
R. Burton	0	1	C. Heafner (3 & 2)
S.L. King	0	1	C. Harbert (4 & 3)
A. Lees	0	1	J. Demaret (7 & 6)
F. Daly	0	1	L. Mangrum (4 & 3)
	5	**7**	

VICTORIOUS CAPTAIN

BEN HOGAN

THE 1950s AND 1960s

1951–1969

1951

Britain's two defeats since the war had served to highlight the widening gap between British and American golf. Bernard Darwin's dispatch on the eve of the match at Pinehurst in North Carolina shows just how far expectations had fallen: 'The British team are facing their task with cheerful optimism that warms the heart, and come what may will acquit themselves well.'

It seemed that Britain faced a hopeless task. Ben Hogan had recovered from his injuries and was back in imperious form, having already collected two Majors that season. And the spine of the American teams that had triumphed in the last two Ryder Cup tournaments was there again for 1951: Sam Snead, Lloyd Mangrum and Jimmy Demaret. In addition, two highly rated new players were brought in, namely 28-year-old Jack Burke and Henry Ransom.

Britain's captain, Arthur Lacey, knew a thing or two about tough Ryder Cup matches. On his debut in 1933, his first match had been against Walter Hagen in the singles. The 1951 team included the bulk of the members from the previous two squads: newly crowned Open Champion Max Faulkner, Rees, Bousfield, Daly, Lees, Ward and Adams. Harry Weetman and John Panton would make their first appearances.

Built in 1907, North Carolina's Pinehurst Country Club was a glorious setting for the ninth Ryder Cup, its famous No. 2 Course measuring just

The Great Britain team aboard the Queen Mary *on their way to compete at Pinehurst Country Club in 1951.*

over 7,000yd. Like Portland in 1947, the weather was wet again, which handed the Americans a further advantage to playing at home.

The Americans out-hit the British pairings on the first day and the matches soon became one-sided. Faulkner and Rees were soundly beaten 5 and 3 by Heafner and new boy Burke, and the Adams/Panton and Daly/Bousfield pairings both lost 5 and 4. It was left to Charlie Ward and Arthur Lees to salvage a bit of pride from the day with a narrow victory over Ed Oliver and Harold Ransom.

The singles proved even more disappointing for the British, with only half a point coming from the first four matches when Fred Daly squared against Clayton Heafner. Dai Rees must have realized that it wasn't his day when his opponent Jimmy Demaret got up and down from ten bunkers during the course of the match. When Lloyd Mangrum beat Harry Weetman 6 and 5, the Cup was officially lost. The remaining four singles matches yielded just one more point for Britain, when Arthur Lees beat Ed Oliver 2 and 1. Ben Hogan brought out the best of Charlie Ward, as the Englishman matched him for the first and much of the second round. But the master holed an enormous putt on the 10th to hold on to his two-shot lead, eventually winning the match on the 16th.

The final score of 9½–2½ was a fair reflection of the American dominance. Despite all the pre-match talk of the American big hitters, it turned out that the more delicate art of putting, especially when under pressure, was the major difference between the two sides. It was a weakness that would come back to haunt the British team two years later.

1951 PINEHURST COUNTRY CLUB, PINEHURST, NORTH CAROLINA

GREAT BRITAIN			UNITED STATES
— FOURSOMES —			
M. Faulkner & D.J. Rees	0	1	C. Heafner & J. Burke (5 & 3)
C.H. Ward & A. Lees (2 & 1)	1	0	E. Oliver & H. Ransom
J. Adams & J. Panton	0	1	S. Snead & L. Mangrum (5 & 4)
F. Daly & K. Bousfield	0	1	B. Hogan & J. Demaret (5 & 4)
— SINGLES —			
J. Adams	0	1	J. Burke (4 & 3)
D.J. Rees	0	1	J. Demaret (2 holes)
F. Daly (halved)	½	½	C. Heafner (halved)
H. Weetman	0	1	L. Mangrum (6 & 5)
A. Lees (2 & 1)	1	0	E. Oliver
C.H. Ward	0	1	B. Hogan (3 & 2)
J. Panton	0	1	S. Alexander (8 & 7)
M. Faulkner	0	1	S. Snead (4 & 3)
	2½	**9½**	

VICTORIOUS CAPTAIN
SAM SNEAD (in 1953)

1953

The match at Wentworth in 1953 evoked memories of the Ryder Cup's birth. Twenty-seven years had elapsed since Abe Mitchell and George Duncan led the British team to a comprehensive victory over Walter Hagen's men on the club's East Course in the first unofficial competition. Since then, the fortunes of the two teams had changed dramatically. Britain had not won the Cup for 18 years and the margins of defeat had become a source of embarrassment. Not only were the Americans producing better golfers, but they had more of them too. The prospects for the British team did not look good at Wentworth, but in the end it proved to be a close contest and would prepare the way for success at Lindrick four years later.

Henry Cotton returned to captain a British team that blended youth with experience. Peter Alliss (son of Percy), Eric Brown, Bernard Hunt and Harry Bradshaw all made their debuts, while Dai Rees, John Panton, Fred Daly, Max Faulkner, Jimmy Adams and Harry Weetman had 15 appearances between them.

As Ben Hogan was unavailable, the United States chose Lloyd Mangrum as captain. He brought with him five new players – Cary Middlecoff, Dale Douglas, Ted Kroll, Fred Haas and Walter Berkemo – while returning were Ed Oliver, Jack Burke, Jim Turnesa and Sam Snead. It was a solid if unspectacular line-up.

Weetman and Alliss teed off first against Douglas and Oliver, and although they fought a close match it was their driving off the tee that let them down. A

ABOVE: *The two captains, Henry Cotton of Great Britain and USA's Lloyd Mangrum, show off the Ryder Cup.*

BELOW: *The United States Ryder Cup team after arriving at London airport. They are (l–r) Lloyd Mangrum (with cup), Dr Cary Middlecoff, Ed Oliver, Sam Snead, Jim Turnesa, Jack Burke, Walter Burkemo, Ted Kroll, Harry Radix, Joe Jemsek, Roy O'Brien (who accompanied the team) and Manager Fred Corcoran.*

topsy-turvy match ended in anticlimax when Weetman, having watched Oliver drive out of bounds, skied his tee shot to leave Alliss no shot to the green. The hole was halved in six and the Americans won 2 and 1.

The two middle matches proved disastrous for Britain, as the Scottish pairing of Brown and Panton lost 8 and 7 to Mangrum and Snead, while Adams and Hunt fared little better, losing 7 and 5 to Kroll and Burke. With their team three points down and with one match left on the course, it fell to Daly and Bradshaw to provide some light on an otherwise grey day. Daly holed out courageously from 10ft on the 36th hole to edge out Burkemo and Middlecoff.

At the end of the first day, and needing six points from eight singles matches, Britain's chances of victory looked non-existent. However, the second day turned out to be one of the tensest finishes in Ryder Cup history. Britain needed a solid start and got one. Going into lunch, the matches were evenly poised – Britain was up in three and all square in two, and Peter Alliss was only one down in his match with Jim Turnesa.

Sam Snead (1912–2002) and Max Faulkner practise before the competition at Wentworth.

When Fred Daly claimed the first British point by defeating Ed Kroll by 9 and 7, attention turned to the lead match between Rees and Burke. This had been a close contest throughout and saw Rees go into the final nine holes one up, only for Burke to square the match on the 13th. Rees then began to fade, and with three putts on the 17th green he handed the match to Burke 2 and 1. Eric Brown beat Lloyd Mangrum on the final hole, while Harry Weetman did the same against Sam Snead, who had squandered a four-hole lead with five holes to play. The score at this stage was 4–4, but it wasn't long before the United States edged ahead to 5–4 when Faulkner lost to Middlecoff 3 and 1.

Three of the four British debutants played in the last three matches. Bradshaw capped a fine debut with a 3 and 2 victory over Fred Haas, leaving the fate of the Ryder Cup in the hands of Peter Alliss and Bernard Hunt. These two players could not have experienced a more tense moment in their young lives and the pressure proved costly. After hitting his drive on the 17th hole out of bounds, Alliss found himself one down going down the last. Alliss then watched Turnesa slice his drive into the trees on the right. Alliss kept his composure and hit a solid drive down the fairway, then hit his second short and to the left. But Turnesa was struggling, eventually finding the green in four. Under pressure from an expectant crowd, Alliss fluffed his third shot, moving the ball just a few inches. His fourth shot was better and left him with a decent chance for par. Turnesa then missed his par putt and finished with a bogey six. Alliss had before him what he would describe as 'one of those' to win the hole and halve the match. But the task was too much, and the point went to the Americans.

With the score at 5–6, it was up to Hunt to salvage a draw for Britain. After fighting back against Douglas on the back nine, Hunt arrived at the 18th tee

BELOW: *A large gallery surrounds the 18th green to watch Sam Snead putt during the opening day foursomes.*

BOTTOM: *Bernard Hunt in practice at Wentworth. For both he and Peter Alliss it would be a debut to forget.*

TOP: *Large crowds watch the singles match between Henry Weetman and Sam Snead at Wentworth. Weetman won by 1 hole.*

ABOVE: *American golfer Fred Haas plays out of a bunker during practice at Wentworth.*

dormie one up. If he could halve the hole, Britain would draw the match. He started well enough with a decent drive, but he sprayed his second right into some trees. His recovery was good though, and the ball rolled up to the back of the green. With two putts for the win, he tried to lag his first putt and left it 4ft short. Like Alliss moments earlier, his second putt slid by the hole. Britain had lost 5½–6½.

Cary Middlecoff plays his approach to the 11th green at Wentworth. Middlecoff beat Max Faulkner 3 and 1.

1953 WENTWORTH GOLF CLUB, VIRGINIA WATER, SURREY

GREAT BRITAIN			UNITED STATES
— FOURSOMES —			
H. Weetman & P. Alliss	0	1	D. Douglas & E. Oliver (2 & 1)
E.C. Brown & J. Panton	0	1	L. Mangrum & S. Snead (8 & 7)
J. Adams & B.J. Hunt	0	1	T. Kroll & J. Burke (7 & 5)
F. Daly & H. Bradshaw (1 hole)	1	0	W. Burkemo & C. Middlecoff
— SINGLES —			
D.J. Rees	0	1	J. Burke (2 & 1)
F. Daly (9 & 7)	1	0	T. Kroll
E.C. Brown (2 holes)	1	0	L. Mangrum
H. Weetman (1 hole)	1	0	S. Snead
M. Faulkner	0	1	C. Middlecoff (3 & 1)
P. Alliss	0	1	J. Turnesa (1 hole)
B.J. Hunt (halved)	½	½	D. Douglas (halved)
H. Bradshaw (3 & 2)	1	0	F. Haas
	5½	**6½**	

VICTORIOUS CAPTAIN

LLOYD MANGRUM

1955

The chance for Peter Alliss and Bernard Hunt to rectify the personal agonies of the final day at Wentworth would have to wait another four years. The combination of a new selection criteria and an unwillingness to risk the young players again meant that they would miss the 1955 trip to the Thunderbird Ranch and Country Club in Palm Springs.

In an attempt to produce a more competitive team, the British PGA had devised a new system of selection based on order of merit. A list of tournaments was drawn up (including the Open Championship), in which players would earn points depending on how well they had performed. The top seven players would then automatically make the Ryder Cup team, with the remaining three players being chosen by the PGA committee.

As a result of the changes, four new players made the team: John Jacobs, Syd Scott, Christy O'Connor and Johnny Fallon, who had finished second behind Peter Thomson at the Open earlier in the summer. On his sixth appearance, Dai Rees assumed the captaincy. Wentworth survivors Eric Brown, Harry Weetman and Harry Bradshaw joined him, with Ken Bousfield and Arthur Lees completing the team.

Chick Harbert was in charge of the American team, which introduced five new players: Tommy Bolt, Marty Furgol, Jerry Barber, Doug Ford and Chandler Harper. Sam Snead, Cary Middlecoff, Ted Kroll and Jack Burke returned from Wentworth.

Located in the Coachella Valley in the shadow of Mt San Jacinto, Thunderbird was, in 1955, one of the most dramatic courses in the United States. The contrast between the flat, lush expanse of grass and the towering desert landscape in the distance is spectacular. With water hazards, narrow fairways and punishing rough, the course provided a unique test for the British team. If that wasn't enough, the greens were in poor shape. The renowned American pitcher and putter Jerry Barber likened them to a piece of asphalt driveway – all bumps, dips and twists. To make matters worse for Britain, the newly crowned PGA Matchplay Champion, Ken Bousfield, had picked up a stomach bug during the practice week and took no part in the match.

Having done their best to acclimatize to the 90°F heat, John Jacobs and Jimmy Fallon led off for Britain in the foursomes, playing a quite magnificent match against Jerry Barber and Chandler Harper. Barber lived up to his reputation by chipping in three times in the morning, leaving the American pair two up at lunch. But after 27 holes the British found themselves one up, Fallon having continued his good putting form. At the 36th hole, and with the British still one up, both teams found the rough off the tee and then ran through the green with their approaches, leaving similar pitches. Harper went first and fluffed his chip, but

*The British Ryder Cup team at
Waterloo Station, London: (back row
l–r) Commander R.C.T. Roe (manager),
Harry Bradshaw, John Jacobs, Dai
Rees, Arthur Lees and Harry Weetman;
(front row l–r) Christy O'Connor, Sid
Scott and Ken Bousfield.*

Jacobs judged his perfectly, leaving it 3ft from the flag. Barber then cleared up his partner's mistake by chipping in, but Fallon made no mistake, holing the putt. The British had their first point.

Brown and Scott had trouble matching Ford and Kroll's scoring in the morning, and it didn't get any better in the afternoon as the American pair ran out 5 and 4 winners. Lees and Weetman were one up on Bolt and Burke at lunch, and managed to cling on for a further nine holes before the Americans won successive holes at the 28th and 29th to go one up. The match went down to the last hole, where both teams faced testing putts. Weetman holed from 11ft, but Burke was equally up to the task and slotted home from 6ft. Bradshaw and Rees were all square after 18 holes and ended up having the best medal score out of all the British pairings, with a total of 136, but Snead and Middlecoff were one shot better and eventually won 3 and 2. Britain had suffered another 3–1 foursomes defeat.

On paper, the results of the singles matches are a little misleading as they suggest that America cruised to an easy victory. But after 30 holes, the British had fought back so much that they might have won; they just couldn't sustain their challenge.

John Jacobs was involved in another 36-hole thriller. Playing Cary Middlecoff, Jacobs started with three birdies and went two up, but Middlecoff was in outstanding form and led by two holes at lunch. Back came Jacobs in the afternoon to square the match after 27 holes. Four holes later, the Briton was two up. Having been forced down the final hole, after Middlecoff holed a massive birdie putt at the 17th, Jacobs coolly holed from 4ft at the last to secure victory. Unofficially, Jacobs shot a 65 in his second round and he had completed a superb debut, but his only playing appearance in the Ryder Cup.

Christy O'Connor had led the team out but found himself three down after 18 holes. He temporarily cut Bolt's lead over him after lunch, but the American soon restored the gap and won comfortably 4 and 2. Rees and Snead had a great battle. Snead was five up at lunch, but Rees produced four birdies in seven holes in the afternoon to reduce the deficit to two holes. Rees kept fighting, but Snead won the 31st hole and eventually ran out a 3 and 1 winner. Harbert managed to repel a recovery from Syd Scott, who at one stage had been six down, and eventually won 3 and 2. Burke and Ford recorded the same margin of victory over Bradshaw and Weetman, respectively. And while Brown and Lees both won their matches, the Americans had already retained the Cup. The match at Thunderbird marked Britain's best score in the United States to date. It also underlined how competitive each individual match could be, even if the overall score was not that close.

1955   THUNDERBIRD GOLF & COUNTRY CLUB, PALM SPRINGS, CALIFORNIA

GREAT BRITAIN			UNITED STATES
— FOURSOMES —			
J. Fallon & J.R.M. Jacobs (1 hole)	1	0	C. Harper & J. Barber
E.C. Brown & S. Scott	0	1	D. Ford & T. Kroll (5 & 4)
A. Lees & H. Weetman	0	1	J. Burke & T. Bolt (1 hole)
H. Bradshaw & D. Rees	0	1	S. Snead & C. Middlecoff (3 & 2)
— SINGLES —			
C. O'Connor	0	1	T. Bolt (4 & 2)
S. Scott	0	1	C. Harbert (3 & 2)
J.R.M. Jacobs (1 hole)	1	0	C. Middlecoff
D.J. Rees	0	1	S. Snead (3 & 1)
A. Lees (3 & 2)	1	0	M. Furgol
E.C. Brown (3 & 2)	1	0	J. Barber
H. Bradshaw	0	1	J. Burke (3 & 2)
H. Weetman	0	1	D. Ford (3 & 2)
4		**8**	

VICTORIOUS CAPTAIN
CHICK HARBERT (in 1949)

1957

Lindrick Golf Club wasn't seen as the most suitable place to upset the American run of victories. The heathland course was thought to be too similar to the courses that the Americans played on week in, week out, and at just over 6,500yd it was too short to test their long hitters. But when Sheffield businessman and Lindrick member Sir Stuart Goodwin agreed to underwrite the cost of staging the contest (gifting the British PGA £10,000), he did so on the condition that the match be held at his home course.

While there weren't any big stars in the American team, they would nonetheless be very difficult to beat. Doug Ford, Dick Mayer and Lionel Hebert had all won Majors that year, and their captain, Jack Burke, had won two the previous year. Tommy Bolt, meanwhile, had proven his skill in matchplay at Thunderbird in 1955.

Of the ten-man British team, Alliss, Brown, Weetman, Hunt, Bradshaw and Faulkner, along with their captain, Dai Rees, had all played in the close match at Wentworth in 1953. Ken Bousfield and Christy O'Connor returned from the team of 1955, and Peter Mills made his debut.

Friday's foursomes began in rather damp, overcast conditions. Alliss and Hunt teed off against Ford and Finsterwald, no doubt looking to erase some of the memories they'd carried from Wentworth four years previously. Although

Dai Rees (1913–83), drives on the 8th tee at Lindrick Golf Club, Yorkshire, during the foursomes on the opening day.

ABOVE: *Doug Ford, Fred Hawkins
and Ed Furgol prepare for practice at
Lindrick.*

RIGHT: *Eric Brown plays out of a
bunker at the 18th during his
tempestuous match with Tommy Bolt,
which the Scot won 4 and 3.*

they were scoring well, the Americans scored better, and in the end it was to their credit that they lost only 2 and 1. Rees and Bousfield had a good 3 and 2 victory over Wall and Hawkins to raise the spirits and tie the match. But soon after the British pair completed their win, the Americans wrapped up the other two matches left on the course. Bolt and Mayer convincingly beat O'Connor and Brown 7 and 5, and Kroll and Burke won their match against Faulkner and Weetman on the 15th green.

Lindrick was a different proposition on the Saturday. The benign conditions of the previous day were replaced by a gusty easterly wind that dried out the course, and an order from the PGA went out to cut the greens as short as was possible to increase their speed.

The United States needed three points from the eight singles matches to retain the Ryder Cup. On six previous occasions they had achieved the figure with ease, securing the trophy with four singles matches still out on the course.

Dai Rees sent out Eric Brown first in what would be a thoroughly tempestuous match with Tommy Bolt. The American was not blessed with the most placid temperament and during his career had picked up his fair share of epithets – Terrible Tommy Bolt, Lightning Bolt, Thunder Bolt to name but a few. His match with Brown only added to his reputation.

Britain's Ken Bousfield plays out of a bunker at the 5th in the second foursomes match on the opening day at Lindrick.

Brown himself was renowned as being an aggressive player and he relished the challenge that Bolt posed. The Briton had arrived at the tournament in good form, having finished third at St Andrew's in the Open Championship earlier in the year.

It wasn't long before Bolt found himself behind in the match. The crowd cheered every one of Brown's successes and each one of Bolt's missed putts, and errant drives were greeted with muted cheers, which only incensed the American even more. The spectators, sensing that they had got to Bolt, continued to hound him quietly and he eventually lost 4 and 3. It had been a bad-tempered affair. Standing on the 18th green, Bolt, referring to the behaviour of the crowd more than anything else, famously remarked to Brown: 'You may have won, but I didn't enjoy that one little bit.' Brown took it personally, saying 'After the whipping I gave you, I wouldn't have enjoyed it either.' A fuming Bolt then walked off the course and promptly broke one of his clubs in frustration. First blood to Great Britain.

Great Britain captain Dai Rees (left) congratulates his foursomes partner Ken Bousfield (right) after the latter sank the winning putt against Art Wall and Fred Hawkins, to earn Britain's only foursomes point.

As the afternoon wore on, it was becoming increasingly clear to an ever more boisterous crowd that the singles matches were going rather well for the home team. Peter Alliss and Harry Bradshaw were in danger of losing their matches (Alliss later did lose 2 and 1), but the rest of the players were on the verge of winning. In the space of an hour, there was a flurry of results. New cap Peter Mills beat American captain Jack Burke 5 and 3, Dai Rees beat Ed Furgol 7 and 6, and Christy O'Connor beat Dow Finsterwald by the same margin. Bernard Hunt conquered his Wentworth demons and coasted to a 6 and 5 victory over Doug Ford, while Bousfield beat Hebert 4 and 3. The wins had arrived in a flood and the Americans didn't know what had hit them. A glance up at the scoreboard would tell them: they had lost the Ryder Cup.

At first the victory was difficult to take in. The speed at which the home team had clinched victory left the crowd not quite believing what they were seeing. From a position of strength at lunchtime, Britain had driven home the advantage in a way that nobody had quite expected. The brilliance of the home team was unquestionable. But what had happened to the Americans? *The Times* golf correspondent suggested a lack of backbone: 'Once they were confronted with the possibility of defeat they collapsed … it was something we do not expect from Americans.'

OPPOSITE PAGE

Members of the victorious British Ryder Cup team chair their captain Dai Rees, as he holds aloft the trophy.

The Americans may well have been guilty of complacency, such was their dominance on the first day. If they had been, they were left with little time to re-engage their brains and turn things around. Britain went to lunch on the final day ahead in five matches. The windy conditions out on the course were not suited to low scoring and the Americans left themselves with too much to do in the remaining 18 holes. Not that the spectators minded – they cheered every putt sunk by the home side.

The jubilant scenes at Lindrick were all the more special for the surprise and speed of the singles victories. Nobody had really expected Great Britain to win, and even if they had, they could not have imagined the scenes that eventually took place. The crowd stayed on in their thousands to witness Dai Rees collect the trophy and describe the day as 'the proudest moment that I've ever had'. A succession of huge cheers greeted the victorious team as Rees was hoisted onto their shoulders, parading the Cup for all the crowd to see. It was a day that would live long in the memory – but then it would have to.

1957 LINDRICK GOLF CLUB, SHEFFIELD, SOUTH YORKSHIRE

GREAT BRITAIN			UNITED STATES
— *FOURSOMES* —			
P. Alliss & B.J. Hunt	0	1	D. Ford & D. Finsterwald (2 & 1)
K. Bousfield & D.J. Rees (3 & 2)	1	0	A. Wall & F. Hawkins
M. Faulkner & H. Weetman	0	1	T. Kroll & J. Burke (4 & 3)
C. O'Connor & E.C. Brown	0	1	R. Mayer & T. Bolt (7 & 5)
— *SINGLES* —			
E.C. Brown (4 & 3)	1	0	T. Bolt
R.P. Mills (5 & 3)	1	0	J. Burke
P. Alliss	0	1	F. Hawkins (2 & 1)
K. Bousfield (4 & 3)	1	0	L. Herbert
D.J. Rees (7 & 6)	1	0	E. Furgol
B.J. Hunt (6 & 5)	1	0	D. Ford
C. O'Connor (7 & 6)	1	0	D. Finsterwald
H. Bradshaw (halved)	½	½	R. Mayer (halved)
	7½	**4½**	

VICTORIOUS CAPTAIN

DAI REES

1959

The dramatic victory at Lindrick had revitalized the Ryder Cup and expectations were high for a good result 1959. 'Britain's best prospects for a quarter of a century,' *The Times* said of the event. But their prospects at Eldorado Country Club in Palm Desert were severely dented by a horrific journey.

In order to foster team spirit, the team had chosen to take the luxury and the time of the *Queen Elizabeth* across the Atlantic rather than fly. But conditions at sea were atrocious and many of the players suffered seasickness. Worse was to follow. Having travelled by train across the country, the players were set to make the last leg of the journey on a short charter flight from Los Angeles over the San Jacinto Mountains to Palm Desert. However, the plane ran into a storm over the mountains and started to judder. Soon it was tilting violently from side to side, then without warning it plunged 5,000ft. All the players were strapped into their seats apart from Bernard Hunt, who had gallantly given his up to the airhostess. As he was standing in the gangway when the plane plunged earthwards, Hunt was thrown up against the roof among flying luggage and sustained bruising and damage to his shoulder. Eventually the plane broke free of the storm and relative calm was restored, only for the pilot to discover that Palm Desert's airport was closed owing to the storm. There was nothing for it but to turn around and fly back to Los Angeles. Safely back on the ground, the players were offered another flight but declined in favour of a Greyhound bus.

When the Britons finally reached Eldorado, they found it tight and, at 6,823yd, long. Like Thunderbird, it had water hazards in front of some of the greens, something of which British golfers had little experience.

At lunch on the opening day, the foursomes were evenly balanced. Although Eric Brown and Bernard Hunt were having a torrid time against Rosberg and Souchak (they were six down), the other matches were well poised – the Americans were one up in two matches, while the British were two up in one. Brown and Hunt ended up losing their match 5 and 4, although Peter Alliss and Christy O'Connor converted their lunchtime advantage into a 3 and 2 victory over Ford and Wall. Rees and Bousfield took their match to the final hole, but couldn't force a half and lost by two holes.

The final foursome should have yielded a full point, but a tactical blunder by Harry Weetman cost Britain dearly. Standing on the 18th fairway one up, all Thomas and Weetman needed to do was to halve the hole. When Sam Snead put the Americans' second shot in the water, victory seemed to be assured. But instead of playing up in front of the water and then simply chipping on for three, Weetman tried for the green. He miscued and the ball landed in the water. With both teams incurring a one-stroke penalty, Thomas and Snead's partner,

Cary Middlecoff, proceeded to chip on to the green for four. Snead made his putt, while Weetman missed his. Instead of finishing the day level, the British were now one point behind, with 1½ points to the Americans' 2½.

The singles results made predictably grim reading for the British, who managed only one win (Eric Brown beat Cary Middlecoff 4 and 3) and two halves (courtesy of Alliss and Drew). Of the five British singles defeats, only Dai Rees, playing against Dow Finsterwald, showed any resistance. At one stage Rees had been 5 down, but rallied heroically to draw level at the 30th hole. But having established parity, Rees quickly fell two behind again at the 33rd and 34th holes. Back came Rees at the 35th, hitting a glorious second shot to within 3ft of the hole. The Welshman duly holed his eagle putt, and took the match down the last. But after looking favourite to win the last hole, when he hit a brilliant iron into the final green, Rees was denied by a beautiful recovery chip from Finsterwald and narrowly lost by 1 hole. The other defeats weren't nearly so close. O'Connor lost 7 and 6 to Wall, and Weetman and Thomas both lost 6 and 5 to Rosberg and Snead respectively. To quote one newspaper, the British had been 'crushed'. This was no exaggeration.

After its two-year sojourn at home, the Ryder Cup passed back into American hands. There was no disgrace in losing to the Americans on their home turf, especially after a journey that had been so fraught, but the sad thing for Britain was that the Americans hadn't yet peaked – Arnie and the boys were waiting just around the corner.

1959 ELDORADO COUNTRY CLUB, PALM DESERT, CALIFORNIA

GREAT BRITAIN			UNITED STATES
— *FOURSOMES* —			
B.J. Hunt & E.C. Brown	0	1	R. Rosberg & M. Souchak (5 & 4)
D.J. Rees & K. Bousfield	0	1	J. Boros & D. Finsterwald (2 holes)
C. O'Connor & P. Alliss (3 & 2)	1	0	A. Wall & D. Ford
H. Weetman & D.C. Thomas (halved)	½	½	S. Snead & C. Middlecoff (halved)
— *SINGLES* —			
N.V. Drew (halved)	½	½	D. Ford (halved)
K. Bousfield	0	1	M. Souchak (3 & 2)
H. Weetman	0	1	R. Rosburg (6 & 5)
D.C. Thomas	0	1	S. Snead (6 & 5)
C. O'Connor	0	1	A. Wall (7 & 6)
D.J. Rees	0	1	D. Finsterwald (1 hole)
P. Alliss (halved)	½	½	J. Herbert (halved)
E.C. Brown (4 & 3)	1	0	C. Middlecoff
	3½	**8½**	

VICTORIOUS CAPTAIN
SAM SNEAD (in 1953)

ABOVE: *The American Ryder Cup team leaving Euston Station, London: (l–r) Jerry Barber, Bill Collins, Gene Littler, Doug Ford, Arnold Palmer, Jay Hebert, Mike Souchait, Dow Finsterwald, Bill Casper and Art Wall.*

OPPOSITE PAGE

TOP LEFT: *Peter Alliss playing from the rough onto the 4th green during the first day.*

TOP RIGHT AND BOTTOM: *Arnold Palmer playing in his first Ryder Cup. Palmer had won his 4th Major championship at Royal Birkdale earlier that year.*

1961

After 34 years and 13 tournaments, it was decided that the format of the Ryder Cup matches should be changed. This would be the start of a long road of minor alterations that would end in 1981, when the format that is played by today's teams was agreed upon. It was by no means a snap decision. Discussions about the format had been going on for some years, but the USPGA and British PGA could never agree on a change. At last, in 1961 a consensus was reached. It was farewell to the marathon 36-hole battles, as four sets of 18 holes would now decide the fate of the Cup. There would be two sets of foursomes – four in the morning, four in the afternoon – on the first day, and two sets of singles – eight in the morning, eight in the afternoon – on the second. There was essentially the same amount of golf, but there would be four sets of pairings for the captains to decide instead of two.

There was much discussion about the new format. With 24 points now at stake instead of 12, who would benefit most? As only 18 holes now decided the fate of a point, would the home team, with their insider's knowledge of the course, have an advantage? Or would the change merely accentuate the greater strength in depth of the American teams? Whatever the changes, Britain still faced an uphill task of reversing the Americans' history of supremacy.

For the 1961 competition, in addition to Ryder Cup regulars Doug Ford, Dow Finsterwald and Art Wall, American captain Jerry Barber had at his disposal some new weapons – Billy Casper, Bill Collins, the graceful Gene Littler and his polar opposite, Arnold Palmer. Palmer was already a superstar when he made his Ryder Cup debut. He was the reigning Open Champion and in the middle of what would be the most prolific period of his career. With his aggressive power off the tee and his wonderfully delicate touch on and around the green, he was the epitome of the saying 'drive for show and putt for dough'. Matchplay was made for him.

If Palmer's much-heralded arrival was a cause for celebration, the premature termination of Sam Snead's Ryder Cup playing career was most certainly not. Earlier that year Snead had entered a non-sanctioned US Tour event and consequently had received a hefty six-month ban. Although this was later

reduced to 45 days, the revision came too late for a distraught Snead. He would not play in the Ryder Cup again.

Dai Rees was in his fourth year as British captain and brought the bulk of the 1959 team with him to Lytham. The selection looked solid if not threatening, with O'Connor, Hunt, Alliss, Weetman and Bousfield, as well as the return of Panton after an eight-year absence. Neil Coles, like Arnold Palmer, began a long Ryder Cup career that year, and Tom Haliburton and Ralph Moffitt completed the British line-up.

In the days of the 12-point matches, Britain had often ended the first day 3–1 down. So, with eight points on offer on the first day, it should have come as no surprise to anyone that they finished 6–2 down on the opening day. O'Connor and Alliss – who would play well all day – got the morning off to a fine start, beating Ford and Littler 4 and 3. But the wheels soon came off as Britain lost the remaining three morning matches. The afternoon promised more than it eventually realized. The O'Connor/Alliss and Haliburton/Coles partnerships both lost at the last hole, and with the other two points shared Britain had a huge task ahead of them.

The highlight of the morning singles matches was the duel between each team's best players, Alliss and Palmer. Alliss maintained a one-hole lead up until the 15th, when Palmer holed out from a greenside bunker to square the match. A nervy final three holes ended with a half point for each player. Rees and Hunt both won, but by claiming five points in the morning the Americans were on the brink of victory, which they duly secured in the first afternoon match. Alliss completed a fine match with a win over Bill Collins, but even three British wins in the final four matches could not disguise another emphatic win for the Americans.

1961 ROYAL LYTHAM & ST ANNES, LANCASHIRE

GREAT BRITAIN			UNITED STATES
— *FOURSOMES* — MORNING			
C. O'Connor & P. Alliss (4 & 3)	1	0	D. Ford & G. Littler
J. Panton & B.J. Hunt	0	1	A. Wall & J. Hebert (4 & 3)
D.J. Rees & K. Bousfield	0	1	W. Casper & A. Palmer (2 & 1)
T.B. Haliburton & N.C. Coles	0	1	W. Collins & M. Souchak (1 hole)
— *FOURSOMES* — AFTERNOON			
C. O'Connor & P. Alliss	0	1	A. Wall & J. Hebert (1 hole)
J. Panton & B.J. Hunt	0	1	W. Casper & A.Palmer (5 & 4)
D.J. Rees & K. Bousfield (2 & 1)	1	0	W. Collins & M. Souchak
T.B. Haliburton & N.C. Coles	0	1	J. Barber & D. Finsterwald (1 hole)
— *SINGLES* — MORNING			
H. Weetman	0	1	D. Ford (1 hole)
R.L. Moffitt	0	1	M. Souchak (5 & 4)
P. Alliss (halved)	½	½	A. Palmer (halved)
K. Bousfield	0	1	W. Casper (5 & 3)
D.J. Rees (2 & 1)	1	0	J. Hebert
N.C. Coles (halved)	½	½	G. Littler (halved)
B.J. Hunt (5 & 4)	1	0	J. Barber
C. O'Connor	0	1	D. Finsterwald (2 & 1)
— *SINGLES* — AFTERNOON			
H. Weetman	0	1	A. Wall (1 hole)
P. Alliss (3 & 2)	1	0	W. Collins
B.J. Hunt	0	1	M. Souchak (2 & 1)
T.B. Haliburton	0	1	A. Palmer (2 & 1)
D.J. Rees (4 & 3)	1	0	D. Ford
K. Bousfield (1 hole)	1	0	J. Barber
N.C. Coles (1 hole)	1	0	D. Finsterwald
C. O'Connor (halved)	½	½	G. Littler (halved)
	9½	**14½**	

VICTORIOUS CAPTAIN

JERRY BARBER

1963

Looking back, it is a relief that the British team only had to make two journeys to the United States in the 1960s. Their first outing at East Lake in Atlanta – home of the legendary Bobby Jones – was, in the end, a dress rehearsal for the more ignominious defeat they would suffer four years later.

After the changes to the match format at Lytham, further tweaking was agreed upon for 1963. For a long time the Americans had wanted to replace the foursome matches, which they thought were rather antiquated, with the more popular fourball format. After much discussion between the two governing bodies, it was agreed that both variations of the game would be included. The contest was also extended to run over three days to increase revenue – one day each for foursomes, fourballs and singles. As a consequence, the total points would jump from 24 to 32. This led Peter Ryde, golf correspondent for *The Times*, to conclude on the eve of the match that this was 'an encouraging aspect … By the end of tomorrow only eight of these points will have been settled. Nothing really decisive will have happened.' The other, more pessimistic, view floating around the press tent was that the increased number of points might serve to highlight the glaring inequalities between the two teams.

The optimists had much to cheer at lunch on the first day, as did the British team. They matched the Americans and shared the points 2–2. Only the solid Lytham pairing of Alliss and O'Connor lost their match, and that was only by a single hole. Despite the good result, British captain Johnny Fallon decided to swap the pairings around for the afternoon matches, with catastrophic results. All four British pairings lost, and any momentum that had been gained at

The United States team at East Lake Country Club 1963: (in white l–r) Arnold Palmer, Tony Lema, Dave Ragan, Dow Finsterwald, Gene Littler, Billy Casper, Robert Goatby, Billy Maxwell and Julius Boros.

lunchtime was abruptly curtailed. It wasn't the best preparation for the new fourballs the next day.

With hindsight, it isn't surprising that the Americans had lobbied so hard for fourball golf. They were good at it – so good, in fact, that they didn't draw or lose the second day of a Ryder Cup for the next 16 years. Although the morning matches ended up being close, the afternoon saw the United States pull ahead, much as they had the previous day. With a score of 12–4 going in to the singles, the prospects of a record defeat looked all too likely.

In light of the chastening experiences of the previous two days, the British performed brilliantly on the third morning, beating the Americans 4½–3½. The most notable performance was Peter Alliss's victory over US captain Arnold Palmer, the pair locking horns again in a match that recalled their ding-dong battle at Lytham. Alliss played beautifully to be two up after 12 holes, but when Palmer fought back at the 16th to take the deficit back to one hole, the crowd started to get excited. Having watched Palmer put his approach shot at the 17th to within 4ft, Alliss now needed to hole his 9ft putt to stay one up. Calmly, at least on the exterior, he did just that. Having weathered the storm, Alliss rolled his ball dead on the last and Palmer

Arnold Palmer and Peter Alliss prepare to play in the morning singles. Alliss recorded a notable one hole victory over Palmer.

was beaten. It was a highpoint of the day and, as Alliss would later recall himself, one of the highpoints of his career.

As the morning matches drew to a conclusion, the Americans needed one point from either of the last two to win the overall tournament. But Bernard Hunt and Harry Weetman managed to stave off defeat until the afternoon, with two final-hole wins.

The inevitable victory arrived with Gene Littler's 6 and 5 win over Tom Haliburton. Only the hero of the morning, Peter Alliss, could muster any British points in the afternoon, claiming a half in his match with Tony Lema.

A final score of 23–9 marked a new low, although it was difficult to see how Britain could have done any better. Johnny Fallon came in for some criticism for chopping and changing his pairings on the first two days, but it would be too harsh to apportion any great blame to one person. American golf was flying high and, as Arnold Palmer rightly remarked, 'This team would beat the rest of the world combined.'

GREAT BRITAIN			UNITED STATES
— FOURSOMES — MORNING			
B. Huggett & G. Will (3 & 2)	1	0	A. Palmer & J. Pott
P. Alliss & C. O'Connor	0	1	W. Casper & D. Ragan (1 hole)
N.C. Coles & B.J. Hunt (halved)	½	½	J. Boros & A. Lema (halved)
D. Thomas & H. Weetman (halved)	½	½	G. Littler & D. Finsterwald (halved)
— FOURSOMES — AFTERNOON			
D. Thomas & H. Weetman	0	1	W. Maxwell & R. Goalby (4 & 3)
B. Huggett & G. Will	0	1	A. Palmer & W. Casper (5 & 4)
N.C. Coles & G.M. Hunt	0	1	G. Littler & D. Finsterwald (2 & 1)
T.B. Haliburton & B.J. Hunt	0	1	J. Boros & A. Lema (1 hole)
— FOURBALLS — MORNING			
B. Huggett & D. Thomas	0	1	A. Palmer & D. Finsterwald (5 & 4)
P. Alliss & B.J. Hunt (halved)	½	½	G. Littler & J. Boros (halved)
H. Weetman & G. Will	0	1	W. Casper & W. Maxwell (3 & 2)
N.C. Coles & C. O'Connor (1 hole)	1	0	R. Goalby & D. Ragan
— FOURBALLS — AFTERNOON			
N.C. Coles & C. O'Connor	0	1	A. Palmer & D. Finsterwald (3 & 2)
P. Alliss & B.J. Hunt	0	1	A. Lema & J. Pott (1 hole)
T.B. Haliburton & G.M. Hunt	0	1	W. Casper & W. Maxwell (2 & 1)
B. Huggett & D. Thomas (halved)	½	½	R. Goalby & D. Ragan (halved)
— SINGLES — MORNING			
G.M. Hunt	0	1	A. Lema (5 & 3)
B. Huggett (3 & 1)	1	0	J. Pott
P. Alliss (1 hole)	1	0	A. Palmer
N.C. Coles (halved)	½	½	W. Casper (halved)
D. Thomas	0	1	R. Goalby (3 & 2)
C. O'Connor	0	1	G. Littler (1 hole)
H. Weetman (1 hole)	1	0	J. Boros
B.J. Hunt (2 holes)	1	0	D. Finsterwald
— SINGLES — AFTERNOON			
G. Will	0	1	A. Palmer (3 & 2)
N.C. Coles	0	1	D. Ragan (2 & 1)
P. Alliss (halved)	½	½	A. Lema (halved)
T.B. Haliburton	0	1	G. Littler (6 & 5)
H. Weetman	0	1	J. Boros (2 & 1)
C. O'Connor	0	1	W. Maxwell (2 & 1)
D. Thomas	0	1	D. Finsterwald (4 & 3)
B.J. Hunt	0	1	R. Goalby (2 & 1)

VICTORIOUS CAPTAIN
ARNOLD PALMER

9   23

1965

US captain Byron Nelson shakes hands with GB captain Harry Weetman.

OPPOSITE PAGE

TOP: *The British Ryder Cup team: (l–r) Peter Butler, Neil Coles, Peter Alliss, Christy O'Connor, George Will, Lionel Platts, Dave Thomas, Jimmy Hitchcock, Jimmy Martin, Bernard Hunt and Harry Weetman (Capt.).*

BOTTOM: *The American Ryder Cup team: (l–r) Byron Nelson (Capt.), Tommy Jacobs, Billy Casper, Don January, Johnny Pott, Tony Lema, Ken Venturi, Dave Marr, Gene Littler, Julius Boros and Arnold Palmer.*

For all the wealth of golfing talent that was on show biennially in the Ryder Cup, behind the scenes there remained the perennial problem of financing the event. Lurching from public whip-rounds and pleas to handouts from philanthropic businessmen with deep pockets, the Ryder Cup had stuttered and stumbled financially from one event to the next. In 1965, at Royal Birkdale, the necessary shot in the arm came from Southport businessman Brian Park, whose donation of £11,000 not only saw that the contest took place, but that it did so in some style.

Park spun together some of the best aspects of American event management with good old-fashioned British hospitality to provide what one commentator described as 'the most ambitious promotion put on in this country'. A vast tented village was erected on the periphery of the course, packed with sponsors' areas, restaurants, bars and children's activities. Journalists were given their own media centre and broadcasters were afforded the best locations for their cameras. Women were employed to drive around in Mini Mokes with a scoreboard attached to the back, so that spectators could be kept up to date. With all the effort that had gone into staging the event, there was, understandably, a touch of unease about how the golf itself would turn out. There was also some worry about the weather, as rain had swept across the course for most of the week leading up to the Thursday start.

Seven of Britain's East Lake team returned to play at Birkdale: Alliss, Hunt, O'Connor, Will, Coles and Thomas, with Weetman as captain. That left space for four new players: Peter Butler, James Martin, Lionel Platts and Jimmy Hitchcock. The Americans, led by Byron Nelson, brought with them Palmer, Lema, Casper, Boros and Littler from the 1963 team, and Ken Venturi, Don January, Dave Marr and Tommy Jacobs.

Britain had a very respectable first day, finishing level at 4–4. Considering what had gone before, this represented one of their best ever starts to the contest. In sustaining a challenge throughout the afternoon, they had kept alive the chance

of staying in touch with the Americans in the dreaded fourballs the following day. The crowd delighted in the temporary dethroning of Arnold Palmer when Thomas and Will gave the great man and Dave Marr a 6 and 5 thrashing. But in the afternoon, Palmer and Marr got their revenge, dishing out the exact same beating to the two Englishmen. Alliss and O'Connor performed flawlessly in both the morning and afternoon, first beating Venturi and January 5 and 4, and then inflicting a 2 and 1 defeat on Casper and Littler. It was at the very end of the day that Bernard Hunt and Neil Coles saw off the challenge of Ken Venturi and Don January on the 16th hole and brought the scores level.

The second day was by no means a disaster, but the Americans pulled away by two points, ending the day on nine points to Britain's seven. It was Alliss and O'Connor's turn to face Palmer and Marr, and although they took a 6 and 4 walloping in the morning in the only match of the day to conclude before the final hole, they came back strongly in the afternoon to win by two holes. As the British team had gained only one point on the second day at East Lake, there was much to praise in their performance at Birkdale. With just the singles to play, technically the Britons were still in with a chance, and over 18 holes who knew what might happen. Realistically, however, it was pride they were playing for.

Befitting all the work Brian Park and his team had put in, the final day was bathed in sunshine from start to finish, which encouraged thousands of spectators through the gates. The Americans forged ahead in the singles, led by comfortable victories by Palmer and Boros. Boros in particular played beautifully, defeating Lionel Platts 4 and 2. Two more victories followed for Lema and Marr, before Bernard Hunt managed to overpower Gene Littler on the final hole for Britain's first point of the day. But points were hard to come by, and Peter Alliss was the only other player to record a win.

The afternoon took on much the same complexion as the morning. Even when Gene Littler had to forfeit the first two holes in his match with George Will because he was carrying 15 clubs instead of 14 (mysteriously, Don January's seven-iron had appeared in his bag), he still won 2 and 1. But by then the match was over. Arnold Palmer had lashed a three-wood from the 18th fairway and his ball trickled on to the green, coming to rest 4ft from the hole. His putt wriggled in and the trophy was won. The final score of Britain 12½, USA 19½ not only reflected the Americans' dominance but also how competitive the British had been.

THE 1950S AND 1960S

1965 ROYAL BIRKDALE GOLF CLUB, SOUTHPORT, MERSEYSIDE

GREAT BRITAIN			UNITED STATES
— FOURSOMES — MORNING			
L. Platts & P.J. Butler	0	1	J. Boros & A. Lema (1 hole)
D.C. Thomas & G. Will (6 & 5)	1	0	A. Palmer & D. Marr
B.J. Hunt & N.C. Coles	0	1	W. Casper & G. Littler (2 & 1)
P. Alliss & C. O'Connor (5 & 4)	1	0	K. Venturi & D. January
— FOURSOMES — AFTERNOON			
D.C. Thomas & G. Will	0	1	A. Palmer & D. Marr (6 & 5)
P. Alliss & C. O'Connor (2 & 1)	1	0	W. Casper & G. Littler
J. Martin & J. Hitchcock	0	1	J. Boros & A. Lema (5 & 4)
B.J. Hunt & N.C. Coles (3 & 2)	1	0	K. Venturi & D. January
— FOURBALLS — MORNING			
D.C. Thomas & G. Will	0	1	D. January & T. Jacobs (1 hole)
L. Platts & P. Butler (halved)	½	½	W. Casper & G. Littler (halved)
P. Alliss & C. O'Connor	0	1	A. Palmer & D. Marr (6 & 4)
B.J. Hunt & N.C. Coles (1 hole)	1	0	J. Boros & A. Lema
— FOURBALLS — AFTERNOON			
P. Alliss & C. O'Connor (2 holes)	1	0	A. Palmer & D. Marr
D.C. Thomas & G. Will	0	1	D. January & T. Jacobs (1 hole)
L. Platts & P.J. Butler (halved)	½	½	W. Casper & G. Littler (halved)
B.J. Hunt & N.C. Coles	0	1	K. Venturi & A. Lema (1 hole)
— SINGLES — MORNING			
J. Hitchcock	0	1	A. Palmer (3 & 2)
L. Platts	0	1	J. Boros (4 & 2)
P.J. Butler	0	1	A. Lema (1 hole)
N.C. Coles	0	1	D. Marr (2 holes)
B.J. Hunt (2 holes)	1	0	G. Littler
D.C. Thomas	0	1	T. Jacobs (2 & 1)
P. Alliss (1 hole)	1	0	W. Casper
G. Will (halved)	½	½	D. January (halved)
— SINGLES — AFTERNOON			
C. O'Connor	0	1	A. Lema (6 & 4)
J. Hitchcock	0	1	J. Boros (2 & 1)
P.J. Butler	0	1	A. Palmer (2 holes)
P. Alliss (3 & 1)	1	0	K. Venturi
N.C. Coles (3 & 2)	1	0	W. Casper
G. Will	0	1	G. Littler (2 & 1)
B.J. Hunt	0	1	D. Marr (1 hole)
L. Platts (1 hole)	1	0	T. Jacobs
	12½	**19½**	

VICTORIOUS CAPTAIN

BYRON NELSON

1967

The match staged at the Champions Golf Club in Houston was an occasion that Britain might care to forget. The team eclipsed its previous record for the heaviest defeat in Ryder Cup history, triggering further discussions about the format of the tournament and its future as a sporting event. It was also the competition at which the Ryder Cup bade farewell to two great servants – Dai Rees and Ben Hogan – and welcomed 23-year-old Tony Jacklin, marking the beginning of his long and glorious association with the contest.

The problems for Britain started even before the tournament had begun. On the eve of the competition, the teams convened for the official pre-match gala dinner. As was traditional, both teams were formally introduced to the assembled guests. The captain of the away team, Dai Rees, went first. One by one he introduced his players, giving a rather long-winded appraisal of their careers thus far. After several minutes of talking, he returned to his seat. In

The United States team: (l–r) Al Geiberger, Julius Boros, Arnold Palmer, Gardiner Dickinson, Ben Hogan (Capt.), Gene Littler, Billy Casper, Johnny Potts, Bobby Nichols, Gay Brewer and Doug Sanders.

stark contrast, Ben Hogan stood up, read out the names of his players one by one, paused, and then said: 'Ladies and gentlemen, the United States Ryder Cup team – the finest golfers in the world.' Hogan's words reverberated around the room and, as the applause got louder, the British team felt that little bit smaller. Hogan's potent words had set the tone for the next three days.

Having made his players feel good about themselves, Hogan then proceeded to tell them who was the boss. It came as no surprise that he approached his final captaincy with dedication and strict discipline – the same way he played his golf – and he expected the same from his players. There were to be no stars in his team and no exceptions to his rule. A good example of Hogan's approach came when he informed Arnold Palmer that all his players would use the smaller 1.62 size British ball instead of the standard US 1.68. On hearing this, Palmer turned to Hogan and said, 'But I don't play the small ball.' 'Who says you're playing?' replied Hogan.

In addition to Palmer, Hogan had at his disposal five other Major champions: Billy Casper, Julius Boros, Gay Brewer, Gene Littler and Al Geiberger. Dai Rees's resources weren't quite so plentiful, but he did have Peter Alliss, Bernard Hunt and Christy O'Connor, who had known what it was like to win a Ryder Cup ten years earlier at Lindrick. Three debutants included Hugh Boyle, Martin Gregson and the rising star of British golf, 23-year-old Tony Jacklin. The competition didn't start too badly for Britain – the 1½ points the players scored on the opening morning wasn't a disgrace. Jacklin, in partnership with Dave Thomas, won comfortably 4 and 3 over Sanders and Brewer, and Huggett and Will halved with Casper and Boros. But from lunch on the first day through to the end of the second, Britain accumulated only a further 1½ points, all from the pairing of Jacklin and Thomas. Three of the matches on day two could have gone either way, with the pairings of Hunt/Coles, Jacklin/Thomas (again) and Will/Boyle all losing at the last hole, but this couldn't disguise the fact that in two days eight British players had contributed just half a point between them. The score was 13–3.

The Americans took the tournament by winning the first three singles matches in the morning, and by lunchtime they had 18 points to Britain's 6. With only 2½ points gained in the afternoon – courtesy of Peter Alliss, Neil Coles and Bernard Hunt – the British team sank to its heaviest defeat: 23½–8½. For once at least, the score told the whole story.

It was some sort of blessing that American television had declined the opportunity to broadcast the contest and that, in the end, only a modest crowd turned up to watch the debacle. For Dai Rees it was a sad end to his Ryder Cup career. But for 54-year-old Hogan, the win capped a wonderful year. He had begun it by shooting a 66 in the third round of the Masters, eventually finishing in tenth place. And he ended it in his home state of Texas, celebrating the most successful performance by an American team in Ryder Cup history.

CHAMPIONS GOLF CLUB, HOUSTON, TEXAS

GREAT BRITAIN			UNITED STATES
— *FOURSOMES* — MORNING			
B.G.C. Huggett & G. Will (halved)	½	½	W. Casper & J. Boros (halved)
P. Alliss & C. O'Connor	0	1	A. Palmer & G. Dickinson (2 & 1)
A. Jacklin & D.C. Thomas (4 & 3)	1	0	D. Sanders & G. Brewer
B.J. Hunt & N.C. Coles	0	1	R. Nichols & J. Pott (6 & 5)
— *FOURSOMES* — AFTERNOON			
B.G.C. Huggett & G. Will	0	1	W. Casper & J. Boros (1 hole)
M. Gregson & H. Boyle	0	1	G. Dickinson & A. Palmer (5 & 4)
A. Jacklin & D.C. Thomas (3 & 2)	1	0	G. Littler & A. Geiberger
P. Alliss & C. O'Connor	0	1	R. Nichols & J. Pott (2 & 1)
— *FOURBALLS* — MORNING			
P. Alliss & C. O'Connor	0	1	W. Casper & G. Brewer (3 & 2)
B.J. Hunt & N.C. Coles	0	1	R. Nichols & J. Pott (1 hole)
A. Jacklin & D.C. Thomas	0	1	G. Littler & A. Geiberger (1 hole)
B.G.C. Huggett & G. Will	0	1	G. Dickinson & D. Sanders (3 & 2)
— *FOURBALLS* — AFTERNOON			
B.J. Hunt & N.C. Coles	0	1	W. Casper & G. Brewer (5 & 3)
P. Alliss & M. Gregson	0	1	G. Dickinson & D. Sanders (3 & 2)
G. Will & H. Boyle	0	1	A. Palmer & J. Boros (1 hole)
A. Jacklin & D.C. Thomas (halved)	½	½	G. Littler & A. Geiberger (halved)
— *SINGLES* — MORNING			
H. Boyle	0	1	G. Brewer (4 & 3)
P. Alliss	0	1	W. Casper (2 & 1)
A. Jacklin	0	1	A. Palmer (3 & 2)
B.G.C. Huggett (1 hole)	1	0	J. Boros
N.C. Coles (2 & 1)	1	0	D. Sanders
M. Gregson	0	1	A. Geiberger (4 & 2)
D.C. Thomas (halved)	½	½	G. Littler (halved)
B.J. Hunt (halved)	½	½	R. Nichols (halved)
— *SINGLES* — AFTERNOON			
B.G.C. Huggett	0	1	A. Palmer (5 & 3)
P. Alliss (2 & 1)	1	0	G. Brewer
A. Jacklin	0	1	G. Dickinson (3 & 2)
C. O'Connor	0	1	R. Nichols (3 & 2)
G. Will	0	1	J. Pott (3 & 1)
M. Gregson	0	1	A. Geiberger (2 & 1)
B.J. Hunt (halved)	½	½	J. Boros (halved)
N.C. Coles (2 & 1)	1	0	D. Sanders
	8½	**23½**	

VICTORIOUS CAPTAIN

BEN HOGAN

The 1969 British Ryder Cup team: (l–r) Brian Huggett, Maurice Bembridge, Alex Caygill, Christy O'Connor, Brian Barnes, Bernard Hunt, Eric Brown (non-playing captain), Peter Alliss, Peter Butler, Tony Jacklin, Neil Coles, Peter Townsend and Bernard Gallacher.

In five decades of competition, the Ryder Cup had played host to some wonderful victories – the first away win by an American team at Ainsdale in 1937, the near whitewash by Ben Hogan's team at Portland Golf Club in 1947, and the dramatic way Dai Rees and his men fought back at Lindrick in 1957. But it was in 1969, at Royal Birkdale, that the Ryder Cup got its first great contest. If only Samuel Ryder could have been there to witness the unfolding drama, he would have been a very proud man indeed.

Previous Ryder Cups had produced their fair share of skill, tactical battles, controversy, sportsmanship, passion and fierce competition. At Royal Birkdale these ingredients came together in a way not seen in the matches before. The events led Peter Ryde of *The Times* to describe the result as 'the most fitting there can ever have been in international matches' and the final scene as 'a climax without blemish'.

Having slumped to a fifth straight defeat and their worst ever losing margin at the Champions Golf Club in 1967, the Britons' chances of winning looked slim. If anything, the Americans, captained by Sam Snead, arrived at Royal Birkdale with a stronger team than in 1967. Jack Nicklaus (winner of seven Major titles already) was included for the first time, and British golf fans would get their first glimpse of emerging stars Lee Trevino and Ray Floyd. The team also included four new faces: Ken Still, Dave Hill, Tommy Aaron and Dan Sikes. Only Billy Casper and Gene Littler had survived from the 1967 team.

With both teams now able to pick 12 players instead of ten (to make the match last a little longer!), Britain had five players who were making their debut: 20-year-old Bernard Gallacher, Brian Barnes, Maurice Bembridge, Peter Townsend and Alex Caygill. Peter Butler returned after playing at Royal Birkdale four years earlier, while the other old hands included Peter Alliss, Brian Huggett, Christy O'Connor, Bernard Hunt and Neil Coles, who between them had made 27 appearances in the Ryder Cup. And, of course, there was Tony Jacklin.

Tony Jacklin had made a respectable Ryder Cup debut in 1967, winning 2½ points for the team, and his talent was clear for all to see. His elegant swing was technically perfect and everyone who saw him play at the Champions Club agreed that he was a player to watch. A year later he won the Greater Jacksonville Open on the USPGA Tour (a rare feat for a Briton even by today's standards), and in

July 1969 he realized his potential and became the first British player in 18 years to win the Open Championship. Jacklin was now one of the best players in the world, and he arrived at Royal Birkdale in top form. A year later he would win the US Open, something no other British player has achieved since. Understandably, the British press was drooling at the prospect of their champion going head to head with the undisputed king of golf, Jack Nicklaus. The Ryder Cup was lucky to have such a contest, and the great men would not let their public down.

Britain began the match well, taking the opening morning foursomes 3½–½. Coles and Huggett ran out 3 and 2 winners over Barber and Floyd, Gallacher and Bembridge beat Trevino and Still 2 and 1, and Jacklin and Townsend comfortably defeated Hill and Aaron 3 and 1. O'Connor and Alliss would secure a half point in their match with Casper and Beard.

All four of the afternoon matches went to the final hole, and all but one of them went the way of the US team. Jack Nicklaus, who had been omitted from the morning foursomes, was sent out in the final pairing of the afternoon. He and his partner, Dan Sikes, spent most of the afternoon in control of their match against Hunt and Butler. But the American pair lost the par-four 16th, when all they could manage was a bogey. All square going down the last, the British pair got an unwelcome reminder of Nicklaus's nerve and skill when, with a deft chip, he provided his partner with an easy tap-in to win the hole and the match.

The pattern that emerged on the first day of competition would set the rules of engagement for the final two days – Britain took the lead in the morning, while the United States fought back in the afternoon. And with 18 of the 32 matches being decided on the final hole, it's not surprising that a few tempers frayed along the way.

On the second day, the morning fourballs went to script as the British players claimed 2½ points and extended their overnight lead by one point (7–5). However, it was events in the afternoon that would steal the newspaper headlines, as the match between Brian Huggett and Bernard Gallacher and the American pairing of Dave Hill and Ken Still turned out to be one of the most controversial in Ryder Cup history.

The match was on the 7th green when the trouble erupted. Hill had been the only player to reach the green in two shots, the rest of them chipping on for three. Hill, being furthest away, was first to putt and rolled his ball to within 2ft of the hole. He then walked up to his ball and tapped it in for a par. His partner, Still, seeing that he couldn't better Hill's score, picked up his ball marker and waited for the British pair to putt out. It was at this point that Gallacher pointed out that Hill had putted out of turn, his ball having been closer to the hole when he putted out than either his or Huggett's balls.

The British pair protested to the match referee that because Hill had played out of turn he should forfeit the hole. The rules of golf were on the side of the British pair, but it is understandable that the Americans felt that they were being petty. The referee had no option but to award the hole to Gallacher and Huggett. Ken Still was furious and remonstrated with the referee, claiming with some justification that this was unsportsmanlike behaviour. When he realized that his protests were futile, he removed Gallacher's ball marker and said: 'You can have the hole and the goddamn Cup'.

The argument rumbled on as they waited to tee off on the 8th. Gallacher continued talking with the officials and Ken Still remained angry. Wanting to get on with the rest of the round, Hill played his tee shot and then wandered over to Gallacher, quietly informing the young man that if he didn't shut up he would get Hill's one-iron wrapped around his neck. By this time the incident had attracted the attention of not only the crowd but also Jack Nicklaus and Dan Sikes (neither of whom was playing that afternoon), PGA President Lord Derby and a number of course officials. The feud was played out silently for the rest of the round, as both teams largely ignored one another. The Americans managed to regain their composure and won on the 17th green 2 and 1.

Moments earlier, Townsend and Butler had lost to Casper and Beard by two holes, which meant that the scores were level at 7–7. In the rapidly fading light of a September evening, the last two matches were halved. After two days of competition the two teams could not be separated.

Britain got off to a poor start in the morning singles with three losses in the first four matches. Only Neil Coles managed a win, beating Tommy Aaron at the last hole. But four wins out of four in the remaining matches, including a resounding 4 and 3 victory for Tony Jacklin over Jack Nicklaus, cheered the mood of the patriotic home crowd. With the score at 13–11, the home team needed only 3½ points out of a remaining eight in the afternoon matches.

Tony Jacklin (left) of Britain and Jack Nicklaus of the United States marking their balls after they had played their shots within inches of each other.

The first six matches in the afternoon were all one-sided affairs. Barnes lost to Hill 4 and 2, Gallacher beat Lee Trevino to win 4 and 3, Bembridge lost to Barber 7 and 6, and Butler won 3 and 2 against Douglass. The home side still needed 1½ points from the remaining four matches. But the Americans fought back, winning the next two matches, which left the score tied at 15–15. With two matches still left out on the course (Huggett vs Casper and Jacklin vs Nicklaus), the match was too close to call.

In his match with Casper, Huggett spent most of the round trailing by one hole. But on the 16th tee Casper pushed his drive into a bunker, and his second shot found the sand too. Huggett kept calm, made sure of his par and won the hole. All square going down the par-five 17th, Casper made birdie and Huggett faced a 7ft putt to halve the hole. Under extraordinary pressure he holed out. They made their way to the 18th tee.

Jacklin strode on to the 17th tee one down, knowing he needed to win one of the last two holes and perhaps both if Britain was to win the Cup. Meanwhile, Huggett and Casper had reached the 18th green in two and were lining up their putts. Casper made a solid birdie four, but Huggett had left himself a testing 4ft putt for the half. As he was settling over his ball, he heard a huge cheer resonate from the direction of the 17th green. Jacklin had holed a 40ft putt to square his match with Nicklaus. The cheers had convinced Huggett that if he holed his putt he would win the Ryder Cup. He stroked the ball home and punched the air with delight. It was only when an emotional Huggett collapsed into the arms of Lord Derby and Eric Brown, who were standing at the back of the 18th green, that he was told it wasn't quite over yet.

Both Jacklin and Nicklaus found the fairway with their final drives, and both had relatively straightforward approach shots to the green. Nicklaus played first and found the right half of the green, some 25ft from the hole. Jacklin fired his ball fractionally to the left of the hole, where it kicked on and finished at the back of the green, leaving him a slightly longer putt.

As the crowds encircled the green, the two men played out the final act. Jacklin was first to putt and left his ball 2ft short. He marked his ball and waited for Nicklaus. Hunched over his ball, Nicklaus gave it a firm tap, knowing that if he holed the putt his team would win. The ball brushed the side of hole but stopped 5ft beyond it. Nicklaus was now left with a similar putt to the one Brian Huggett had faced moments before, and like Huggett he made no mistake.

Jacklin still needed to hole out, but Nicklaus didn't give him the chance. He bent down, picked up Jacklin's marker and went over to shake his hand. As the two men put their arms around one another, Nicklaus famously remarked: 'I don't think you would have missed that putt Tony, but in the circumstances I would never give you the opportunity.'

An historic moment in Ryder Cup matches: Jack Nicklaus and Tony Jacklin shake hands after squaring the final singles match. Nicklaus conceded Jacklin's 2ft putt to hand Britain a draw.

It was a fitting finale to a quite extraordinary contest, although US captain Sam Snead didn't quite see it like that – he would have preferred Jacklin to have putted out. But Nicklaus's gesture would define the spirit of the Ryder Cup, which at times during the previous two days had been put to the test. In front of an adoring crowd Jacklin had proved himself a true champion, leading the way by winning five points of his team's total of 16.

1969 ROYAL BIRKDALE GOLF CLUB, SOUTHPORT, MERSEYSIDE

GREAT BRITAIN			UNITED STATES
— *FOURSOMES* — MORNING			
N.C. Coles & B.G.C. Huggett (3 & 2)	1	0	M. Barber & R. Floyd
B. Gallacher & M. Bembridge (2 & 1)	1	0	L. Trevino & K. Still
A. Jacklin & P. Townsend (3 & 1)	1	0	D. Hill & T. Aaron
C. O'Connor & P. Alliss (halved)	½	½	W. Casper & F. Beard (halved)
— *FOURSOMES* — AFTERNOON			
N.C. Coles & B.G.C. Huggett	0	1	D. Hill & T. Aaron (1 hole)
B. Gallacher & M. Bembridge	0	1	L. Trevino & G. Littler (1 hole)
A. Jacklin & P. Townsend (1 hole)	1	0	W. Casper & F. Beard
P.J. Butler & B.J. Hunt	0	1	J. Nicklaus & D. Sikes (1 hole)
— *FOURBALLS* — MORNING			
C. O'Connor & P. Townsend (1 hole)	1	0	D. Hill & D. Douglass
B.G.C. Huggett & G.A. Caygill (halved)	½	½	R. Floyd & M. Barber (halved)
B. Barnes & P. Alliss	0	1	L. Trevino & G. Littler (1 hole)
A. Jacklin & N.C. Coles (1 hole)	1	0	J. Nicklaus & D. Sikes
— *FOURBALLS* — AFTERNOON			
P.J. Butler & P. Townsend	0	1	W. Casper & F. Beard (2 holes)
B.G.C. Huggett & B. Gallacher	0	1	D. Hill & K. Still (2 & 1)
M. Bembridge & B.J. Hunt (halved)	½	½	T. Aaron & R. Floyd (halved)
A. Jacklin & N.C. Coles (halved)	½	½	L. Trevino & M. Barber (halved)
— *SINGLES* — MORNING			
P. Alliss	0	1	L. Trevino (2 & 1)
P. Townsend	0	1	D. Hill (5 & 4)
N.C. Coles (1 hole)	1	0	T. Aaron
B. Barnes	0	1	W. Casper (1 hole)
C. O'Connor (5 & 4)	1	0	F. Beard
M. Bembridge (1 hole)	1	0	K. Still
P.J. Butler (1 hole)	1	0	R. Floyd
A. Jacklin (4 & 3)	1	0	J. Nicklaus
— *SINGLES* — AFTERNOON			
B. Barnes	0	1	D. Hill (4 & 2)
B. Gallacher (4 & 3)	1	0	L. Trevino
M. Bembridge	0	1	M. Barber (7 & 6)
P.J. Butler (3 & 2)	1	0	D. Douglass
N.C. Coles	0	1	D. Sikes (4 & 3)
C. O'Connor	0	1	G. Littler (2 & 1)
B.G.C. Huggett (halved)	½	½	W. Casper (halved)
A. Jacklin (halved)	½	½	J. Nicklaus (halved)

16   16

VICTORIOUS CAPTAIN

SAM SNEAD (in 1953)

THE 1970s

1971–1979

FOR ALL THE GRINDING MONOTONY OF THE OVERALL MATCH RESULTS in the 1970s, it did, in the end, provide the catalyst for a much needed discussion about the format of the Ryder Cup. The game the British Isles had exported had finally been perfected by the Americans, but as it turned out, the 1970s would be the last decade in which the United States would completely dominate Major championship golf. While the overall result of the Ryder Cup was rarely in doubt, the individual contests often produced exciting golf that thrilled the spectators. This and the underlying sense of cordiality between the two teams was, and still is, as important as winning the Cup itself. But the Cup needed a contest or it would fade into obscurity, and by the end of decade all the people that mattered wanted to see a change.

1971

The drawn match at Royal Birkdale had revitalized what had been a flagging contest. But while the British public relished seeing their players take on the superstars of American golf, hoping against hope that they would fell a sporting Goliath, the American public hadn't been so keen to watch a team of British professionals turn up on American soil and get thrashed. The exciting climax to the 1969 contest, coupled with Tony Jacklin's victory at the US Open the previous summer, altered that opinion. The potential for another close encounter persuaded American broadcasters to televise the event nationally for the first time.

The prospect of a close contest was also enthusing Eric Brown, who retained the captaincy of the British team. He observed that the Old Warson Country Club in St Louis, Missouri, had many of the characteristics of the courses back home – rolling ground, narrowish fairways and tight drives. Rather cheekily, he suggested that the British were happier with the course set-up than the Americans. But if the course was to his players' liking, the weather most certainly wasn't – on the practice days leading up to the match, the temperature was touching 90°F.

Nine of Britain's Birkdale team returned in 1971, the remaining three places being filled by Peter Oosterhuis, Harry Bannerman and John Garner, who all made their debuts. The Americans fielded six players from Birkdale. Arnold Palmer and Gardner Dickinson returned from the team of 1967, and future captain Dave Stockton made his first Cup appearance. The team's only concern was over the fitness of Lee Trevino, who had recently undergone an appendix operation.

Despite all the pre-match talk of how hot it was, on the first morning the players were greeted with a deluge of rain. The extravagant opening ceremony had to be postponed and play eventually got underway an hour and a quarter late. The fresher conditions suited the visitors, and Britain went into an early 3–1 lead after the morning foursomes. Then was Birkdale revisited after lunch, as the Americans staged a comeback. However, this wasn't enough to stop Britain taking a 4½–3½ lead into day two – their best ever start away from home.

Any parallels with the match at Birkdale ended abruptly on the second morning, when the Americans claimed all four points. None of the matches reached the final hole and journalists were left scratching their heads as to why the Jacklin/Huggett pairing hadn't been utilized.

TOP: *The British Ryder Cup Team: (l–r) Eric Brown (Capt.), Brian Huggett, Brian Barnes, Peter Oosterhuis, Peter Townsend, Bernard Gallacher, Peter Butler, Christy O'Connor, Tony Jacklin, Maurice Bembridge, John Garner and Harry Bannerman.*

ABOVE: *Members of the GB team at practice at the South Herts Golf Club.*

The Americans' most convincing win of the morning fourballs was that of Palmer and Dickinson, who overcame Gallacher and Oosterhuis comfortably 5 and 4. The match was notable for a bizarre incident that led to the British pair to forfeit the 7th hole. Having watched Palmer hit his tee shot on to the green, Gallacher's caddie then casually asked him what club he had taken. Palmer replied, saying he had used a five-iron. However, the rules of golf strictly prohibit such questions, as they could be deemed as an attempt to gain an unfair advantage, and the referee, who overheard the exchange, immediately awarded the hole to the Americans. Palmer felt the decision was a bit harsh, and to his credit tried to get it reversed. But the referee held firm and the decision stood.

Britain fared a little better in the afternoon but still only managed 1½ points compared to the Americans' 6½. As a result, the United States had turned a one-point deficit into a four-point lead (10–6). The match was slipping away and everyone in the British team knew it.

Early the next morning, news filtered through that Billy Casper had contrived to break a toe in the night while trying to get to his hotel bathroom. He would not play in the singles. But for the British there still lay a daunting task ahead – they needed 10½ points from the 16 on offer.

Britain made a decent start, with Barnes beating Rudolph by one hole and Oosterhuis beating Littler 4 and 3, but they fell away in the remaining morning matches, managing only 3½ points out of 8. The United States now needed only two more points in the afternoon to win the Cup. Trevino and Snead delivered in the first two matches. At that point the score was 16½–9½. Britain went on to win four of the remaining six matches (Oosterhuis beating Palmer 3 and 2 was the highlight), giving the final result of 18½–13½ more respectability. Although it was also Britain's best ever result on American soil, the damage done on a catastrophic second day had been too much to repair.

In his post-match interviews, Eric Brown focused on the positives. However, the British journalists were frustrated by his upbeat comments and, when he refused to elaborate on the strategy he had employed on the second morning, which took the match away from Britain, he was roundly criticized and consequently was not invited back to captain the team again.

Bad captaincy or not, the Americans were simply too good. The new television audience may well have concluded that Birkdale was a blip and that normal service had been resumed.

September 1971: 22-year-old Bernard Gallacher practises at South Herts Golf Club before the team flew to America to compete at the Old Warson Country Club, Missouri.

1971 OLD WARSON COUNTRY CLUB, ST LOUIS, MISSOURI

GREAT BRITAIN			UNITED STATES
FOURSOMES — MORNING			
N.C. Coles & C. O'Connor (2 & 1)	1	0	W. Casper & M. Barber
P. Townsend & P. Oosterhuis	0	1	A. Palmer & G. Dickinson (1 hole)
B.G.C. Huggett & A. Jacklin (3 & 2)	1	0	J. Nicklaus & D. Stockton
M. Bembridge & P.J. Butler (1 hole)	1	0	C. Coody & F. Beard
FOURSOMES — AFTERNOON			
H. Bannerman & B. Gallacher (2 & 1)	1	0	W. Casper & M. Barber
P. Townsend & P. Oosterhuis	0	1	A. Palmer & G. Dickinson (1 hole)
B.G.C. Huggett & A. Jacklin (halved)	½	½	L. Trevino & M. Rudolph (halved)
M. Bembridge & P.J. Butler	0	1	J. Nicklaus & J.C. Snead (5 & 3)
FOURBALLS — MORNING			
C. O'Connor & B. Barnes	0	1	L. Trevino & M. Rudolph (2 & 1)
N.C. Coles & J. Garner	0	1	F. Beard & J.C. Snead (2 & 1)
P. Oosterhuis & B. Gallacher	0	1	A. Palmer & G. Dickinson (5 & 4)
P. Townsend & H. Bannerman	0	1	J. Nicklaus & G. Littler (2 & 1)
FOURBALLS — AFTERNOON			
B. Gallacher & P. Oosterhuis (1 hole)	1	0	L. Trevino & W. Casper
A. Jacklin & B.G.C. Huggett	0	1	G. Littler & J.C. Snead (2 & 1)
P. Townsend & H. Bannerman	0	1	A. Palmer & J. Nicklaus (1 hole)
N.C. Coles & C. O'Connor (halved)	½	½	C. Coody & F. Beard (halved)
SINGLES — MORNING			
A. Jacklin	0	1	L. Trevino (1 hole)
B. Gallacher (halved)	½	½	D. Stockton (halved)
B. Barnes (1 hole)	1	0	M. Rudolph
P. Oosterhuis (4 & 3)	1	0	G. Littler
P. Townsend	0	1	J. Nicklaus (3 & 2)
C. O'Connor	0	1	G. Dickinson (5 & 4)
H. Bannerman (halved)	½	½	A. Palmer (halved)
N.C. Coles (halved)	½	½	F. Beard (halved)
SINGLES — AFTERNOON			
B.G.C. Huggett	0	1	L. Trevino (7 & 6)
A. Jacklin	0	1	J.C. Snead (1 hole)
B. Barnes (2 & 1)	1	0	M. Barber
P. Townsend	0	1	D. Stockton (1 hole)
B. Gallacher (2 & 1)	1	0	C. Coody
N.C. Coles	0	1	J. Nicklaus (5 & 3)
P. Oosterhuis (3 & 2)	1	0	A. Palmer
H. Bannerman (2 & 1)	1	0	G. Dickinson
	13½	**18½**	

VICTORIOUS CAPTAIN
JAY HEBERT (in 1961)

1973

For the first time in 46 years, the Ryder Cup made its way to Scotland – the venue in 1973 was Muirfield. Only a year earlier the club had been the scene of heartbreak for Tony Jacklin, when Lee Trevino chipped in at the 71st hole (to add to three previous ones) and went on to retain the Open Championship. It had moved golf commentator Henry Longhurst to pronounce that he had 'never seen so many diabolical flukes thrown at a man'.

With players from the Republic of Ireland now available for selection, there was much hope that the new Great Britain and Ireland team could repeat the performance at Birkdale in 1969 or even go one better, and everyone agreed that Jacklin could once again prove to be the inspiration for a stirring performance from the British and Irish side. But it was a trick he would be unable to repeat. Although Jacklin was still one of the finest players in the world, Trevino had dealt a fatal blow to his confidence and he would not win another Major championship in his career.

Brian Barnes had also played well at that Open Championship, finishing fifth – his best ever result in a Major – and with the return of a strong contingent of the Birkdale team, including Bembridge, Gallacher, Huggett, O'Connor, Butler and Coles, there was a feeling of quiet optimism. However, the Americans were now producing some of their strongest teams in the history of the Ryder Cup. Jack Nicklaus had overtaken the great Walter Hagen's haul of 11 Major victories by winning the USPGA Championship a month earlier, Lee Trevino was in the middle of his purple patch, and Palmer, Casper, Aaron and Brewer were all still world-class players. Add the reigning US Open Champion Tom Weiskopf, plus Lou Graham, Homero Blancas and Chi Chi Rodriguez (all rookies), and it was difficult to see the weak link.

It was therefore something of a surprise and a delight, when after two days of matches the home side found themselves back where they were in 1969, level at 8–8. A strong set of afternoon fourballs (the foursomes and fourballs were now played alternately) on the opening day consolidated the lead they had achieved in the morning. All three afternoon points came from

Jack Nicklaus: in 1973 the 'Golden Bear' overtook Walter Hagen's haul of 11 majors by winning the USPGA Championship at Canterbury Golf Club in Ohio.

comfortable wins, the pick being Bembridge and Huggett's 3 and 1 victory over Palmer and Nicklaus. After sharing the points 2–2 in the morning foursomes on day two, it was disappointing that Britain and Ireland managed only half a point in the afternoon, when one win would have given them their first lead going into a final day since Ganton in 1949.

The singles matches would not live up to the drama at Birkdale, as the Americans recorded three important victories at the top of the card. Casper, Weiskopf and Blancas were all comfortably home before the 18th hole against Barnes, Gallacher and Butler, respectively. The rest of the points in the morning were shared – Bembridge, who had the misfortune to draw Jack Nicklaus in both his singles matches, gained a marvellous half point after being two down with three to play.

The afternoon started and ended well. Huggett had a 4 and 2 win over Blancas, and Oosterhuis kept his unbeaten record in singles matches by winning against Arnold Palmer by the same margin. However, the games in between these two yielded only half a point. Playing in his last Ryder Cup, 48-year-old Christy O'Connor halved his match with Tom Weiskopf, but the rest of the team struggled. A more aggressive Nicklaus defeated Maurice Bembridge by two holes, and Gallacher and Coles were both thrashed 6 and 5 by Brewer and Trevino. When Jacklin, who had played so well in the morning, went down to Billy Casper in the middle of the afternoon, the tournament was officially over. The final result – Great Britain and Ireland 13, the United States 19.

Overall, the British and Irish team had performed well. Maurice Bembridge, who was on recall to the team and faced Jack Nicklaus four times out of six, played exceptionally well to win a creditable three points. As before, however, the Americans had found an extra gear when they needed it. Prime Minister Edward Heath presented the trophy to American captain Jack Burke, and the teams looked forward to their next meeting at Laurel Valley.

1973 MUIRFIELD, EAST LOTHIAN

GREAT BRITAIN AND IRELAND			UNITED STATES
— FOURSOMES — MORNING			
B.W. Barnes & B.J. Gallacher (1 hole)	1	0	L. Trevino & W.J. Casper
C. O'Connor & N.C. Coles (3 & 2)	1	0	T. Weiskopf & J.C. Snead
A. Jacklin & P. Oosterhuis (halved)	½	½	J. Rodriguez & L. Graham (halved)
M. Bembridge & P.J. Butler	0	1	J.W. Nicklaus & A. Palmer (6 & 5)
— FOURBALLS — AFTERNOON			
B.W. Barnes & B.J. Gallacher (5 & 4)	1	0	T. Aaron & G. Brewer
M.E. Bembridge & B.G.C. Huggett (3 & 1)	1	0	A. Palmer & J.W. Nicklaus
A. Jacklin & P. Oosterhuis (3 & 1)	1	0	T. Weiskopf & W.J. Casper
C. O'Connor & N.C. Coles	0	1	L. Trevino & H. Blancas (2 & 1)
— FOURSOMES — MORNING			
B.W. Barnes & P.J. Butler	0	1	J.W. Nicklaus & T. Weiskopf (1 hole)
P. Oosterhuis & A. Jacklin (2 holes)	1	0	A. Palmer & D. Hill
M.E. Bembridge & B.G.C. Huggett (5 & 4)	1	0	J. Rodriguez & L. Graham
N.C. Coles & C. O'Connor	0	1	L. Trevino & W. Casper (2 & 1)
— FOURBALLS — AFTERNOON			
B.W. Barnes & P.J. Butler	0	1	J.C. Snead & A. Palmer (2 holes)
A. Jacklin & P. Oosterhuis	0	1	G. Brewer & W. Casper (3 & 2)
C. Clark & E. Polland	0	1	J.W. Nicklaus & T. Weiskopf (3 & 2)
M.E. Bembridge & B.G.C. Huggett (halved)	½	½	L. Trevino & H. Blancas (halved)
— SINGLES — MORNING			
B.W. Barnes	0	1	W.J. Casper (2 & 1)
B.J. Gallacher	0	1	T. Weiskopf (3 & 1)
P.J. Butler	0	1	H. Blancas (5 & 4)
A. Jacklin (3 & 1)	1	0	T. Aaron
N.C. Coles (halved)	½	½	G. Brewer (halved)
C. O'Connor	0	1	J.C. Snead (1 hole)
M.E. Bembridge (halved)	½	½	J.W. Nicklaus (halved)
P. Oosterhuis (halved)	½	½	L. Trevino (halved)
— SINGLES — AFTERNOON			
B.G.C. Huggett (4 & 2)	1	0	H. Blancas
B.W. Barnes	0	1	J.C. Snead (3 & 1)
B.J. Gallacher	0	1	G. Brewer (6 & 5)
A. Jacklin	0	1	W.J. Casper (2 & 1)
N.C. Coles	0	1	L. Trevino (6 & 5)
C. O'Connor (halved)	½	½	T. Weiskopf (halved)
M.E. Bembridge	0	1	J.W. Nicklaus (2 holes)
P. Oosterhuis (4 & 2)	1	0	A. Palmer

VICTORIOUS CAPTAIN

JACK BURKE (in 1953)

13   19

1975

As had happened in 1965 at Royal Birkdale, heavy rain preceded the match at Laurel Valley Golf Club in Pennsylvania, which made a long course (ten holes were more than 430yd) much longer. This would again suit the American team, which had the longer hitters – not that they needed any help. Although a resurgent Gary Player had managed to unfurl a South African flag among a sea of Stars and Stripes in 1974, winning the Masters and the Open, there was no getting away from the fact that since 1970 American players had won 20 out of 24 Majors.

The American team couldn't have been more relaxed. For non-playing captain Arnold Palmer, whose house was just a few miles up the freeway, it was something of a home-from-home competition. Nicklaus, who arrived late, was left to organize his own practice. Notable debuts were made by Hale Irwin and Johnny Miller, and Raymond Floyd returned after a six-year absence.

To liven up the proceedings (and to encourage spectators through the gates), the organizers had scheduled a pro-celebrity match the day before the Ryder Cup was due to start. Peter Ryde of *The Times* was not amused: 'We are threatened with a celebrity pro-am match tomorrow, involving the rival captain and, inevitably, Bob Hope. I dislike the idea of dressing up this match which should stand or fall on its own quality and tradition.'

Tradition was something the British had in spades. Quality, however, was not quite so plentiful among the Great Britain and Ireland team. It did include Tony Jacklin, but even by 1975 it was generally agreed that his greatest playing days were well behind him. Six new players were blooded that year. Two of them – Eamonn Darcy and Christy O'Connor Jr (the nephew of the departing Christy O'Connor Sr) – would go on to record career highlights in the Ryder Cup, but of Tommy Horton, Guy Hunt, John O'Leary and Norman Wood, only Horton would appear in Cup matches again. Aside from Jacklin, experience came in the form of Gallacher, Barnes, Bembridge, Oosterhuis and Brian Huggett (who played for his sixth and final time).

Brian Barnes, with his pipe in his mouth, blasts out of a sand trap during the match at Laurel Valley Golf Club, Ligonier, Pa. Barnes beat Jack Nicklaus twice on the final day of the competition, 4 and 2 in the morning, and 2 and 1 in the afternoon.

It was with predictable ease that the Americans whitewashed Britain and Ireland in the morning foursomes. It seemed that Arnold Palmer's rather ambitious hope of winning all 32 matches wasn't looking quite so ridiculous. Mercifully, Britain scraped 1½ points in the afternoon: Jacklin and Oosterhuis beat Casper and Floyd 2 and 1, and Barnes and Gallacher shared a point with Nicklaus and Murphy.

Things didn't improve much on the second day either, with Britain and Ireland managing just two points. Jacklin and his two different partners – Oosterhius in the morning and Barnes in the afternoon – took 1½ points, while Darcy and Hunt claimed their first points in a Ryder Cup. That aside, the day was another disaster, with all the American wins confirmed by the time they reached the 16th green. The day had ended 6–2 in favour of the United States, who led 12½–3½ overall. It was a miserable scoreline for the British and Irish to contemplate, and was their second-lowest two-day tally since the fourballs were introduced in 1963. And with the Americans' history of strong singles matches, captain Bernard Hunt's mind must have drifted back to the Champions Club in Houston, when he was a member of the team that lost by 15 points. Although the game was lost by lunchtime on the final day, an absorbing sideshow did emerge in the form of a battle between Brian Barnes and Jack Nicklaus.

On day three it fell to Tom Weiskopf to deliver the point that sealed the Americans' victory, closing out Guy Hunt 5 and 3 shortly before lunch. But it was the match going on behind them that would steal the headlines that day. Brian Barnes was a good golfer, but his opponent, Jack Nicklaus, was the best player the world had ever seen. So when Barnes beat Nicklaus 4 and 2 in the morning it was thought that Nicklaus, knowing that American victory was guaranteed, hadn't taken the match as seriously as he would have should the overall competition have been close. With the press clamouring to interview Barnes at lunchtime, team captains Bernard Hunt and Arnold Palmer contrived to pair them together again in the afternoon.

If Nicklaus had been coasting in the morning, he made it abundantly clear that he meant business in the afternoon. On arrival at the 1st tee, he greeted Barnes, saying 'Well done this morning, Barnesy, but there's no way you're gonna beat me this afternoon.'

Nicklaus promptly won the first two holes, but Barnes hung on and stopped the gap widening further. Gradually he turned the match around, and with a birdie at the 17th beat Nicklaus 2 and 1 to record a memorable double over the world no.1. As ever, the great man himself – as commentator Henry Longhurst used to call him – was courteous in defeat, even though underneath it all he was fuming.

In the end, the victory margin was ten points at 21–11, a defeat to rival the lows of the 1960s. Calls to widen the scope of selection were repeated but the British PGA was still resistant. One more bad result would force them to change their mind.

1975   LAUREL VALLEY GOLF CLUB, LIGONIER, PENNSYLVANIA

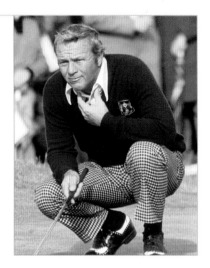

VICTORIOUS CAPTAIN
ARNOLD PALMER (in 1973)

GREAT BRITAIN AND IRELAND			UNITED STATES
FOURSOMES — MORNING			
B.W. Barnes & B.J. Gallacher	0	1	J.W. Nicklaus & T. Weiskopf (5 & 4)
N. Wood & M. Bembridge	0	1	G. Littler & H. Irwin (4 & 3)
A. Jacklin & P. Oosterhuis	0	1	A. Geiberger & J. Miller (3 & 1)
T. Horton & J. O'Leary	0	1	L. Trevino & J.C. Snead (2 & 1)
FOURBALLS — AFTERNOON			
P. Oosterhuis & A. Jacklin (2 & 1)	1	0	W.J. Casper & R. Floyd
E. Darcy & C. O'Connor Jr	0	1	T. Weiskopf & L. Graham (3 & 2)
B.W. Barnes & B.J. Gallacher (halved)	½	½	J.W. Nicklaus & R. Murphy (halved)
T. Horton & J. O'Leary	0	1	L. Trevino & H. Irwin (2 & 1)
FOURBALLS — MORNING			
P. Oosterhuis & A. Jacklin (halved)	½	½	W.J. Casper & J. Miller (halved)
T. Horton & N. Wood	0	1	J.W. Nicklaus & J.C. Snead (4 & 2)
B.W. Barnes & B.J. Gallacher	0	1	G. Littler & L. Graham (5 & 3)
E. Darcy & G.L. Hunt (halved)	½	½	A. Geiberger & R. Floyd (halved)
FOURSOMES — AFTERNOON			
A. Jacklin & B.W. Barnes (3 & 2)	1	0	L. Trevino & R. Murphy
C. O'Connor Jr & J. O'Leary	0	1	T. Weiskopf & J. Miller (5 & 3)
P. Oosterhuis & M. Bembridge	0	1	H. Irwin & W.J. Casper (3 & 2)
E. Darcy & G.L. Hunt	0	1	A. Geiberger & L. Graham (3 & 2)
SINGLES — MORNING			
A. Jacklin	0	1	R. Murphy (2 & 1)
P. Oosterhuis (2 holes)	1	0	J. Miller
B.J. Gallacher (halved)	½	½	L. Trevino (halved)
T. Horton (halved)	½	½	H. Irwin (halved)
B.G.C. Huggett	0	1	G. Littler (4 & 2)
E. Darcy	0	1	W.J. Casper (3 & 2)
G.L. Hunt	0	1	T. Weiskopf (5 & 3)
B.W. Barnes (4 & 2)	1	0	J.W. Nicklaus
SINGLES — AFTERNOON			
A. Jacklin	0	1	R. Floyd (1 hole)
P. Oosterhuis (3 & 2)	1	0	C. Snead
B.J. Gallacher (halved)	½	½	A. Geiberger (halved)
T. Horton (2 & 1)	1	0	L. Graham
J. O'Leary	0	1	H. Irwin (2 & 1)
M. Bembridge	0	1	R. Murphy (2 & 1)
N. Wood (2 & 1)	1	0	L. Trevino
B.W. Barnes (2 & 1)	1	0	J.W. Nicklaus
	11	**21**	

1977

The 50th anniversary of the Ryder Cup saw a fourth change to the format, the first since those made in the early 1960s. Royal Lytham & St Annes had hosted the first contest to be decided by more than 12 points back in 1961, and in 1977 it was the venue for a second experiment that ended up being a failed attempt to make the match more competitive. Like the Great Britain and Ireland team it wouldn't survive the match, but the principal for all future singles matches was established, whereby each player would play one 18-hole match instead of two on the final day.

The game was notable for the debuts of two golfing legends. On the American team was Tom Watson, who had already secured one Masters title and two Open Championships (his latest, at Turnberry in the famous 'Duel in the Sun' contest with Jack Nicklaus, had taken place only two months earlier during a parched July). The British and Irish, meanwhile, included 20-year-old Nick Faldo who would go on to compete in a record 11 contests and win more Ryder Cup points (25) than any other player.

Lining up behind Faldo in the Britain and Ireland team were some more names of the future: Ken Brown, Mark James and Howard Clark, who all began their Ryder Cup journeys at Lytham. Back on the team for the eighth and final time was Neil Coles. He didn't win a match in 1977, but he had served his side and the Ryder Cup with distinction for 16 years. Barnes, Gallacher, Horton, Oosterhuis, Darcy and Jacklin all kept their places, and Brian Huggett was appointed captain.

Ken Brown and Mark James discuss headgear during their fourballs match against Hale Irwin and Lou Graham on the second day. The British pair lost by 1 hole.

BELOW LEFT: *Hale Irwin and Brian Barnes at the par-three 5th hole. Barnes beat Irwin by 1 hole in the singles.*

BELOW: *Jack Nicklaus, a study in concentration.*

Dow Finsterwald's United States team included Lanny Wadkins for the first time. The British public would only get a glimpse of him – such were the margins of his three victories that Wadkins didn't have to play the 18th all weekend. Dave Stockton made his first appearance overseas, US Open Champion Hubert Green debuted, and some familiar names showed up too, including Jack Nicklaus, Ray Floyd and Dave Hill.

Even with fewer matches Britain and Ireland lost heavily, taking only 2½ points from the first two days. In the singles they fared much better, squaring 5–5 with the Americans. Curiously, there were no halved matches in the singles, which hadn't happened

since 1955. The final score of 7½–12½ looks closer than it was, but there were many positives for Britain and Ireland.

Peter Oosterhuis maintained his unbeaten run in singles matches, and his new partnership with Nick Faldo in the foursomes and fourballs gelled immediately. They both won all their matches, contributing four points to the total of 7½. Nick Faldo beat Tom Watson in the singles, and Bernard Gallacher recorded what he described as his greatest ever win, beating Jack Nicklaus by one hole. Having been four up after four holes, Gallacher then watched in vain as Nicklaus chipped away at his lead. The match was squared at the 16th, but then Gallacher holed an 80ft putt on the 17th for birdie and, as he put it, 'squeezed home' down the last.

Royal Lytham & St Annes marked the end of an era in Ryder Cup matches. The Great Britain and Ireland defeat finally forced the British PGA into action – two years later the Cup would witness its slow rebirth.

OPPOSITE PAGE

TOP LEFT: *Nick Faldo and Peter Oosterhuis who together contributed 4 of GB & Ireland's 7½ points.*

TOP RIGHT: *Tony Jacklin was omitted from the final day's singles matches.*

BOTTOM: *United States Captain Dow Finsterwald, surrounded by his team, proudly raises the Ryder Cup.*

1977 ROYAL LYTHAM & ST ANNES, LANCASHIRE

VICTORIOUS CAPTAIN
DOW FINSTERWALD

GREAT BRITAIN AND IRELAND			UNITED STATES
— *FOURSOMES* —			
B.J. Gallacher & B.W. Barnes	0	1	L. Wadkins & H. Irwin (3 & 1)
N.C. Coles & P. Dawson	0	1	D. Stockton & M. McGee (1 hole)
N. Faldo & P. Oosterhuis (2 & 1)	1	0	R. Floyd & L. Graham
E. Darcy & A. Jacklin (halved)	½	½	E. Sneed & D. January (halved)
T. Horton & M. James	0	1	J.W. Nicklaus & T. Watson (5 & 4)
— *FOURBALLS* —			
B.W. Barnes & T. Horton	0	1	T. Watson & H. Green (5 & 4)
N.C. Coles & P. Dawson	0	1	E. Sneed & L. Wadkins (5 & 3)
N. Faldo & P. Oosterhuis (3 & 1)	1	0	J.W. Nicklaus & R. Floyd
A. Jacklin & E. Darcy	0	1	D. Hill & D. Stockton (5 & 3)
M. James & K. Brown	0	1	H. Irwin & L. Graham (1 hole)
— *SINGLES* —			
H. Clark	0	1	L. Wadkins (4 & 3)
N.C. Coles	0	1	L. Graham (5 & 3)
P. Dawson (5 & 4)	1	0	D. January
B.W. Barnes (1 hole)	1	0	H. Irwin
T. Horton	0	1	D. Hill (5 & 4)
B.J. Gallacher (1 hole)	1	0	J.W. Nicklaus
E. Darcy	0	1	H. Green (1 hole)
M. James	0	1	R. Floyd (2 & 1)
N. Faldo (1 hole)	1	0	T. Watson
P. Oosterhuis (2 holes)	1	0	J. McGee
	7½	**12½**	

1979

*The first European team to contest
the Ryder Cup: (back row l–r) Mark
James, Sandy Lyle, Nick Faldo, Peter
Oosterhuis, Antonio Garrido and
Bernard Gallacher; (front row l–r) Des
Smyth, Ken Brown, Tony Jacklin, John
Jacobs (Capt.), Seve Ballesteros, Brian
Barnes and Michael King.*

A quick leaf through the history books reveals that the US team won the 23rd Ryder Cup by the comfortable margin of 17–11. It would be their tenth victory in 11 attempts since their defeat at Lindrick, but the match played at the Greenbrier, West Virginia, in 1979 was a landmark for the competition. For the first time, players from Continental Europe were considered for Ryder Cup selection, and it was hoped that their participation might produce a closer contest and challenge the Americans' dominance. But what was to be a historic occasion for the newly formed European team would also turn out to be something of a histrionic affair.

The idea of something other than a Great Britain and Ireland team challenging the United States had first been advanced in the wake of the defeat at Royal Lytham & St Annes two years earlier. Speaking to the press after the US victory, Jack Nicklaus expressed a widely held concern that the competition was in danger of losing its prestige and meaning if it continued to be such a one-sided affair. Nicklaus was keen on the idea of broadening the scope of players who could be considered for selection and mentioned that the Great Britain and Ireland team might be extended to include players from Europe. It wasn't long before Nicklaus was engaged in conversation with PGA President

Lord Derby. Derby, it seemed, was all for the idea. After batting around some less convenient geographical bounds (English-speaking countries and Commonwealth nations were both considered), the PGA sensibly settled on a European course.

The European Tour had been established in 1971. A year later, in its first full season, players from around Europe competed in 20 tournaments, eight of them hosted outside Britain. The professionals wanted to play in the competitions and spectators would arrive in good numbers to watch them. When 19-year-old Seve Ballesteros burst on to the world golf scene in 1976, finishing second in the Open Championship at Royal Birkdale, the tour had its first celebrity. Ballesteros's success generated an interest in other Spanish players on the tour (including Manuel Piñero, Antonio Garrido and José-Maria Canizares) and would pave the way for future European talent. The USPGA Tour might have been much older and richer, but with stars like Seve around the European Tour could only get bigger and better.

So it was that in the spring of 1978 Brian Huggett and Peter Butler (members of the British Ryder Cup Committee) flew to the US to seek the approval of the USPGA for Great Britain and Ireland to compete as Europe. The approval was granted. The revitalization this decision would give to the contest in future years couldn't have been imagined.

The first European team to contest the Ryder Cup consisted of six Englishmen, three Scots, an Irishman and two Spaniards – Severiano Ballesteros and Antonio Garrido. The Spaniards' contributions to the actual competition were small (together they would win only one point in six matches), but their involvement and presence were symbolic of a new era for the Ryder Cup.

From left to right: Bernard Gallacher, Sandy Lyle, Brian Barnes and Ken Brown.

Not so impressive were the contributions of two young players on the European team, Ken Brown and Mark James. Gifted though they may have been, they were also cursed/blessed (depending on how you want to look at it) with a rebellious streak. Problems began to surface before they even boarded the flight to the United States. While the rest of the team assembled at Heathrow Airport smartly dressed in regulation suit and tie, the pair sauntered into the terminal wearing casual clothes. This incident would set the tone for the whole trip. Once they had arrived in West Virginia, Brown and James missed a team meeting in favour of doing a spot of shopping, and at the opening ceremony they both looked as if it was the last place on earth they wanted to be.

When the match finally got underway on Friday morning, European captain John Jacobs, in a historic gesture, sent Ballesteros and Garrido out first against Lanny Wadkins and Larry Nelson. Thinking it was best to keep trouble confined to one match, he sent Brown and James out together second. Oosterhuis and Faldo followed, with Gallacher and Barnes last. It was a poor start for the Europeans, who managed only one point.

They fared little better in the afternoon fourballs, although Ballesteros and Garrido did win their first Ryder Cup point, defeating Fuzzy Zoeller and Hubert Green 2 and 1. Meanwhile, Tony Jacklin and Sandy Lyle managed to share a point with Lee Trevino and Gil Morgan.

However, the day was marred by the antics of James and, in particular, Brown. Having lost the morning foursome to Trevino and Zoeller, it was then revealed that James had a chest-muscle injury. He would take no further part in the match. With James absent, Brown was paired with Des Smyth for the afternoon fourballs. Brown totally ignored his playing partner throughout the match, which in the event didn't last very long as they were thrashed 7 and 6 by Hale Irwin and Tom Kite.

A difficult first day for the Europeans ended with them three points adrift of the United States. But by the end of the second day, minus Brown and James, they had fought back well. The gap going into the singles matches was just a single point.

A promising start by Bernard Gallacher on the final morning (a 3 and 2 winner over Lanny Wadkins) was then wiped out by five straight wins for the Americans. Three of the five matches were tight (Jacklin, Garrido and Barnes all took their matches to the final hole), but the Ryder Cup had been lost again. The six afternoon singles brought wins for Irwin, Green and Trevino, along with a winning margin that was all too familiar.

The first ever match between Europe and the United States had been an interesting one, but for all the wrong reasons. Brown's behaviour earned him a ban and James was given a £1,500 fine. The pair did, however, go on to restore their reputations and both represented Europe again. Brown would be a member of the Ryder Cup teams that made history in 1985 and 1987, before injury forced him into premature retirement when he was in his early 30s. James played a further five times for Europe and would eventually go on to captain the European Ryder Cup team at the infamous Brookline match in 1999.

BELOW: *Bernard Gallacher and Brian Barnes, who won three out of four of their matches together.*

BOTTOM: *The winning United States team.*

1979 THE GREENBRIER, WEST VIRGINIA

	EUROPE	UNITED STATES	

— FOURBALLS — MORNING

	EUROPE	UNITED STATES	
A. Garrido & S. Ballesteros	0	1	L. Wadkins & L. Nelson (2 & 1)
K. Brown & M. James	0	1	L. Trevino & F. Zoeller (3 & 2)
P. Oosterhuis & N. Faldo	0	1	A. Bean & L. Elder (2 & 1)
B. Gallacher & B. Barnes (2 & 1)	1	0	H. Irwin & J. Mahaffey

— FOURSOMES — AFTERNOON

	EUROPE	UNITED STATES	
K. Brown & D. Smyth	0	1	H. Irwin & T. Kite (7 & 6)
S. Ballesteros & A. Garrido (3 & 2)	1	0	F. Zoeller & H. Green
A. Lyle & A. Jacklin (halved)	½	½	L. Trevino & G. Morgan (halved)
B. Gallacher & B. Barnes	0	1	L. Wadkins & L. Nelson (4 & 3)

— FOURSOMES — MORNING

	EUROPE	UNITED STATES	
A. Jacklin & A. Lyle (5 & 4)	1	0	L. Elder & J. Mahaffey
N. Faldo & P. Oosterhuis (6 & 5)	1	0	A. Bean & T. Kite
B. Gallacher & B. Barnes (2 & 1)	1	0	F. Zoeller & M. Hayes
S. Ballesteros & A. Garrido	0	1	L. Wadkins & L. Nelson (3 & 2)

— FOURBALLS — AFTERNOON

	EUROPE	UNITED STATES	
S. Ballesteros & A. Garrido	0	1	L. Wadkins & L. Nelson (5 & 4)
A. Jacklin & A. Lyle	0	1	H. Irwin & T. Kite (1 hole)
B. Gallacher & B. Barnes (3 & 2)	1	0	L. Trevino & F. Zoeller
N. Faldo & P. Oosterhuis (1 hole)	1	0	L. Elder & M. Hayes

— SINGLES — MORNING

	EUROPE	UNITED STATES	
B. Gallacher (3 & 2)	1	0	L. Wadkins
S. Ballesteros	0	1	L. Nelson (3 & 2)
A. Jacklin	0	1	T. Kite (1 hole)
A. Garrido	0	1	M. Hayes (1 hole)
M. King	0	1	A. Bean (4 & 3)
B. Barnes	0	1	J. Mahaffey (1 hole)

— SINGLES — AFTERNOON

	EUROPE	UNITED STATES	
N. Faldo (3 & 2)	1	0	L. Elder
D. Smyth	0	1	H. Irwin (5 & 3)
P. Oosterhuis	0	1	H. Green (2 holes)
K. Brown (1 hole)	1	0	F. Zoeller
A. Lyle	0	1	L. Trevino (2 & 1)
M. James (injured, DNP)	½	½	G. Morgan (DNP)

11	**17**

VICTORIOUS CAPTAIN

BILLY CASPER

THE 1980s

1981–1989

1981

On paper, the tournament played at Walton Heath, Surrey, in 1981 looked to be a total mismatch – the American team arrived in Britain boasting nine Major championship winners (only Bruce Lietzke would fail to win one in his career), while the Europeans currently had none. And so it proved to be come the final day, as the Americans surged ahead in the newly convened singles matches. Up until lunchtime on the Saturday – exactly halfway through the competition – Europe did, however, give the United States a bit of a fright.

If the final result wasn't controversial, the build-up to the match most certainly was. Seve Ballesteros, who had represented the inaugural European team in the 1979 Ryder Cup tournament in West Virginia, was available for selection again. Victories at the Open Championship in 1979 and the Masters in 1980 had made him a superstar, and with this success came the opportunity to play more golf on the lucrative USPGA Tour. As a consequence, Ballesteros had not earned enough money on the European Tour to qualify automatically. His selection for the team would be decided by the PGA panel whose job it was to pick the final two players.

Ballesteros's place seemed assured until a much publicized row erupted over his demands to be paid appearance money. It was European Tour policy not to pay players appearance money and the selectors held firm against the Spaniard's request. Ballesteros stuck to his guns, arguing that because he would add to the gate receipts he should receive an appearance fee. With little chance of a compromise, Europe captain John Jacobs asked Ballesteros if would play in two tournaments before the selection of the team was finalized so that he might qualify automatically. Ballesteros refused and so was not selected.

Equally controversial was the omission of Tony Jacklin. Although Jacklin was now 37 years old and was considered to be past his best, his commitment to the Ryder Cup and his record in matches had been excellent. When Jacobs told him that his place had gone to Ryder Cup bad boy Mark James instead, Jacklin was hurt by the snub and vowed never to get involved in Ryder Cup tournaments again.

THE 1980s

In time, the hoo-ha surrounding the non-selection of these two players proved beneficial to the European team. When Jacklin reversed his decision to quit and returned as captain in the 1983 team, his genuine sympathy for Ballesteros's point of view would prove vital in persuading the emotional Spaniard to rejoin the team.

As if all this wasn't enough, the original venue – the Belfry, which was the new headquarters of the British PGA – had to be changed at short notice because its recently constructed Brabazon Course was considered unfit for tournament play. Having been completed only four years before, the course was still bedding in and needed more time to mature. Ex-Ryder Cup player Brian Barnes had described it as resembling a ploughed field. Walton Heath, one of a number of scenic heathland courses in Surrey, was chosen as its replacement.

Although John Jacobs fielded a relatively inexperienced European team, he had, in 32-year-old Bernard Gallacher, the most experienced Ryder Cup player on either side. Nick Faldo, Eamonn Darcy, Peter Oosterhuis, Des Smyth, Sandy Lyle, Mark James and Howard Clark also all had previous Cup experience. Sam Torrance made his Ryder Cup debut, as did two Spaniards – skilled matchplayer Manuel Piñero and 34-year-old José-Maria Canizares. The final place went to 24-year-old rookie Bernhard Langer, whose growing reputation had been boosted not only by a second place to Bill Rogers at the Open Championship, but also by famously playing his ball out of a tree at the Benson and Hedges International Open at Fulford a few weeks earlier.

The United States team-sheet, as Tom Kite would later comment, was like 'a *Who's Who* of world golf at that time'. Jack Nicklaus, Tom Watson, Lee Trevino, Ray Floyd, Johnny Miller, Jerry Pate and Hale Irwin had all been Major champions, and Bill Rogers and Larry Nelson had won their first Major championships earlier in the year. Future captain Ben Crenshaw and Bruce Lietzke, meanwhile, were making their Ryder Cup debuts.

The points in the foursomes on the opening morning were shared, the pick of the wins for Europe being a good 3 and 2 for Gallacher and Smyth over Irwin and Floyd. Faldo and Oosterhuis had the thankless task of trying to contain the irresistible combination of Nicklaus and Watson; they couldn't, and went down 4 and 3.

Jack Nicklaus and Tom Watson discuss the line of a putt in their opening foursomes match against Nick Faldo and Peter Oosterhuis at Walton Heath. The Americans won the match 4 and 3.

For the afternoon fourball matches Jacobs kept the pairing of Lyle and James, who went on to beat Crenshaw and Pate 3 and 2 in the second match out. Torrance and Clark shared a point with Kite and Miller, so that when Des Smyth and José-Maria Canizares destroyed Rogers and Lietzke 6 and 5, the overall score read Europe 4½, USA 2½. Gallacher and Darcy fought hard against Floyd and Irwin, but eventually they shook hands on the 17th green having lost 2 and 1. The disappointment of losing this final match could hardly dampen the spirits of the European players, who went back to their hotel happy and surprised at their one-point lead.

Any sense of nervousness that the Europeans had going into the second-day matches must have intensified when they opened their morning newspapers – suddenly, expectation abounded. Spectators who had funnelled through the gates to catch a glimpse of their American heroes were now starting to believe that the Europeans might put up a decent challenge, or, dare they even think it, win the Ryder Cup.

Those hopes were beginning to fade by lunchtime. Faldo and Torrance had tamely surrendered 7 and 5 to Trevino and Pate, and only Langer and Piñero, 2 and 1 victors over Floyd and Irwin, managed to deliver a point for Europe. The afternoon brought no respite. The Americans effectively seized their chance to

Lee Trevino watches his partner Larry Nelson tee-off in the opening day foursomes. The American pair beat Bernhard Langer and Manuel Piñero by 1 hole.

Tom Watson plays out of a bunker on a rain-affected second day at Walton Heath.

kill the match and executed four comfortable victories in the foursomes. Not one of these matches made it to the final green. As the light faded, the spectators filed off the course and were left to ponder their disappointment on a day that had started with such optimism.

The Americans were all but out of sight going into the singles matches, with 10½ points to Europe's 5½, and Sunday proved to be another brutal day for the home team. The United States took the four points they needed from the first five matches and the competition was officially won. The second match, between Tom Kite and Sandy Lyle, was an extraordinary spectacle of target golf. When Kite closed out Lyle 3 and 2 on the 16th green, he was unofficially at ten under par. Lyle was only two shots behind, on eight under par. If the spectators couldn't enjoy the result, they could certainly enjoy the golf.

Europe did manage three wins in the singles, the most notable being Howard Clark's 4 and 3 victory over reigning Masters Champion Tom Watson, but the tournament was long over. At the end of the day they lost the singles eight points to four.

In the immediate aftermath, the European players must have felt like the stuffing had been knocked out them. After the first day the US team had won 15 points out of the 20 on offer and had savaged their opponents. American captain Dave Marr suggested that the Europeans had made a tactical mistake in taking the lead on the first day, saying that it had hurt the Americans and awakened them to their responsibilities. However, the final scoreline of 18½–9½ indicated a bigger gulf in talent between the teams than there actually was, and the American dominance of the previous 20 years was slowly being chipped away. The European Tour had begun to nurture not only some very talented players but some doughty ones too.

1981 WALTON HEATH GOLF CLUB, SURREY

VICTORIOUS CAPTAIN
DAVE MARR

	EUROPE	UNITED STATES	
FOURSOMES — MORNING			
B. Langer & M. Piñero	0	1	L. Trevino & L. Nelson (1 hole)
A. Lyle & M. James (2 & 1)	1	0	B. Rogers & B. Lietzke
B. Gallacher & D. Smyth (3 & 2)	1	0	H. Irwin & R. Floyd
P. Oosterhuis & N. Faldo	0	1	T. Watson & J. Nicklaus (4 & 3)
FOURBALLS — AFTERNOON			
S. Torrance & H. Clark (halved)	½	½	T. Kite & J. Miller (halved)
A. Lyle & M. James (3 & 2)	1	0	B. Crenshaw & J. Pate
D. Smyth & J.-M. Canizares (6 & 5)	1	0	B. Rogers & B. Lietzke
B. Gallacher & E. Darcy	0	1	H. Irwin & R. Floyd (2 & 1)
FOURBALLS — MORNING			
N. Faldo & S. Torrance	0	1	L. Trevino & J. Pate (7 & 5)
A. Lyle & M. James	0	1	L. Nelson & T. Kite (1 hole)
B. Langer & M. Piñero (2 & 1)	1	0	R. Floyd & H. Irwin
J.-M. Canizares & D. Smyth	0	1	J. Nicklaus & T. Watson (3 & 2)
FOURSOMES — AFTERNOON			
P. Oosterhuis & S. Torrance	0	1	L. Trevino & J. Pate (2 & 1)
B. Langer & M. Piñero	0	1	J. Nicklaus & T. Watson (3 & 2)
A. Lyle & M. James	0	1	B. Rogers & R. Floyd (3 & 2)
D. Smyth & B. Gallacher	0	1	T. Kite & L. Nelson (3 & 2)
SINGLES			
S. Torrance	0	1	L. Trevino (5 & 3)
A. Lyle	0	1	T. Kite (3 & 2)
B. Gallacher (halved)	½	½	B. Rogers (halved)
M. James	0	1	L. Nelson (2 holes)
D. Smyth	0	1	B. Crenshaw (6 & 4)
B. Langer (halved)	½	½	B. Lietzke (halved)
M. Piñero (4 & 2)	1	0	J. Pate
J.-M. Canizares	0	1	H. Irwin (1 hole)
N. Faldo (2 & 1)	1	0	J. Miller
H. Clark (4 & 3)	1	0	T. Watson
P. Oosterhuis	0	1	R. Floyd (1 hole)
E. Darcy	0	1	J. Nicklaus (5 & 3)
	9½	**18½**	

1983

The 1983 tournament, held at the PGA National Golf Club in Florida, proved to be the turning point for the European team and the prelude to a glorious era for the Ryder Cup. Although no one knew it yet, the depressing run of crushing American victories was over, and the seemingly bottomless pit of American golfing talent was going to be tested. While even a win on home soil still seemed unlikely, victory in the United States would be nothing less than a sensation.

After his fallout with PGA officials over his omission from the Walton Heath side, it surprised everyone that Tony Jacklin accepted the captaincy of the European team. Having been approached about the job by European Tour Director Ken Schofield prior to teeing off at the Car Care Plan Tournament at Sandmoor in May earlier that year, Jacklin said he would go away and think about it. Four hours and 65 shots later, he agreed to take on the role. However, his acceptance came with conditions.

Jacklin had long thought that the European team's preparations for the competitions had been inadequate. While the Americans enjoyed first-class travel, accommodation and clothing, the Europeans had to make do with slumming it across the Atlantic in tourist class, checking in at two-star accommodation, and donning cheap polyester blazers and inferior kit – Jacklin's standard-issue plastic shoes had fallen apart on the course at Laurel Valley in 1975. 'It was', Jacklin argued, 'as if the team were two down before they arrived on the first tee.' He wanted the players to be treated like sporting ambassadors, reasoning that if they looked and felt the part they had a much greater chance of playing the part. Every request was granted.

But before the team left for the United States, Jacklin had to persuade Seve Ballesteros to rejoin it after his controversial omission at Walton Heath in 1981. Jacklin went to visit the Spaniard at the Open Championship in July, and over breakfast at the Prince of Wales Hotel in Southport he told him that things had changed. He said that the players would be treated properly now and, most importantly, that the European team needed him. Jacklin had to wait two weeks for an answer, but it was the one he wanted. Ballesteros was back on board.

Concorde duly delivered the European players, along with their wives and caddies (another Jacklin demand), to the United States. Europe was now

Members of the European team stand beside Concorde, dressed in their tailor-made blazers. Tony Jacklin demanded that his team receive the first-class treatment.

OPPOSITE PAGE

TOP: *The opening ceremony at PGA National Golf Club, Palm Beach, Florida.*

BOTTOM: *The European team: (back row l–r) Ian Woosnam, Paul Way, Bernhard Langer, Bernard Gallacher and Sam Torrance; (front row l–r) Gordon J. Brand, Ken Brown, Brian Waites, Tony Jacklin (Capt.), Nick Faldo, Sandy Lyle and Seve Ballesteros.*

producing high-quality players and in Ballesteros it probably had the best player in the world at that time. Faldo, Langer, Lyle and Woosnam were all turning into champions, and José-Maria Canizares, Sam Torrance, Ken Brown and Bernard Gallacher were also quality professionals. In addition, Jacklin took three rookies with him: Brian Waites, Gordon J. Brand and 20-year-old Paul Way.

Seve Ballesteros hits his astonishing three-wood from the fairway bunker at the 18th when playing Fuzzy Zoeller.

OPPOSITE PAGE

TOP: *Lanny Wadkins is congratulated by his team-mates after playing the pitch shot of his life at the 18th to secure victory for the United States.*

BOTTOM: *The winning United States team: (standing l–r) Craig Stadler, Jay Haas, Gil Morgan, Bob Gilder, Jack Nicklaus (Capt.), Tom Watson, Ray Floyd, Curtis Strange and Fuzzy Zoeller; (front l–r) Tom Kite, Ben Crenshaw, Calvin Peete and Lanny Wadkins.*

Captained by Jack Nicklaus, the United States team had in five times Open Champion Tom Watson one of the greatest pressure players of all time. Lanny Wadkins was a reputed matchplayer, Fuzzy Zoeller and Ben Crenshaw were a year away from winning Majors, and Craig Stadler had won the Masters at Augusta the previous year. However, the eccentricities of the US selection criteria meant that there were a couple of notable omissions from their squad, namely the reigning US Open and USPGA Champions, Larry Nelson and Hal Sutton.

After a poor start in the opening foursome match – Gallacher and Lyle crashed to a 5 and 4 defeat to Watson and Crenshaw – Europe fought back, and at lunchtime the team was level with the United States on two points each. Faldo and Langer (who would drop only one point between them all tournament) were comfortable 4 and 2 winners over Wadkins and Stadler, and Canizares and Torrance beat Ray Floyd and Bob Gilder 4 and 3. After losing his first match in partnership with Paul Way, Ballesteros wanted to join his compatriot Canizares for the afternoon fourballs, but Jacklin took Seve aside and told him that he wanted him to mentor Way, to guide and inspire him. The pair didn't lose thereafter.

Concerned about the form of both Lyle and Gallacher, Jacklin dropped them for the afternoon fourballs in favour of Ken Brown and Brian Waites. The new pairing delivered a vital point. In fact, only Faldo and Langer failed to score in the afternoon, which left the Europeans leading by one point at the end of day one on 4½–3½. Jacklin was already leaving his mark on the team.

On the second morning the Americans drew level, taking 2½ points to make the score 6–6. Faldo and Langer won their match against Peete and Crenshaw 4 and 2, and Ballesteros and Way snatched a half. By the end of the day, the teams were locked together on even points (8–8), the first time this had happened in the United States. It had been ten years since parity had been achieved heading into the singles matches. Jacklin had played that year, and had watched the Americans run away with the match in the morning singles.

Jacklin handed his playing order for the singles to the officials. His three best players – Ballesteros, Faldo and Langer – would go out first. This was a gamble and Jacklin knew it. Nicklaus, on the other hand, adopted a more conventional strategy, putting his best players out last.

Jacklin's gamble pretty much paid off. Europe gained 2½ points out of a possible three from the first three matches – Faldo beat Haas 2 and 1, and Langer won on the 18th against Morgan. Ballesteros managed to halve his match with Zoeller, and achieved that only by playing one of the most audacious shots ever seen in a Ryder Cup. Standing on the 18th tee, the players were all square. Ballesteros then drove into rough that was so thick he could move his ball only 20yd forward. It found a fairway bunker, leaving him 240yd to the green. He then pulled out his three-wood and caught the ball perfectly, so that it landed just 20ft from the hole. Jack Nicklaus reckoned that, given the circumstances, it was the best stroke he'd ever seen.

Europe gained one point (Paul Way beat Curtis Strange 2 and 1) from the following four matches, putting the scores level at 11½ each. Torrance then produced a wonderful pitch from the rough on the 18th to halve his match with Tom Kite, and Ken Brown ended what had been a dismal Ryder Cup for Raymond Floyd by beating him 4 and 3. When Woosnam lost to Stadler 3 and 2, the match score was level at 13 points each.

That left two matches out on the course: Tom Watson was playing Bernard Gallacher and José-Maria Canizares against Lanny Wadkins. At this point, the match was heading for a draw. Watson was in a strong position in his match, and Canizares led Wadkins. However, as they drove off the 18th tee Wadkins had a chance to halve the match and effectively win the Ryder Cup.

Canizares's third shot to the 18th green drifted to the right and was short. Wadkins knew he had a chance. With lightning storms flashing all around him, he executed an exquisite pitch, floating the ball to within 15in of the hole. He later described it as 'the most pressure I have ever felt in making one shot'. His team-mates hurried over to congratulate him, and Jack Nicklaus walked over to the spot from where Wadkins had struck his ball. Crouching down, he placed a kiss on the divot. The relief was palpable.

For a dejected European team there was much to ponder: putts that had shaved the hole, half points that had slipped away, and the feeling of coming so close to beating the USA in its own backyard. But in truth, there was much they could be positive about. They had made the Ryder Cup a real contest for the first time in 14 years, and Jacklin's

demands and approach to the captaincy had been vindicated. The European Tour was now producing world-class golfers and next time around Europe had the home advantage. The disappointment of 1983 would soon turn to joy.

1983 PGA NATIONAL GOLF CLUB, PALM BEACH GARDENS, FLORIDA

EUROPE			UNITED STATES
FOURSOMES — MORNING			
B. Gallacher & A. Lyle	0	1	T. Watson & B. Crenshaw (5 & 4)
N. Faldo & B. Langer (4 & 2)	1	0	L. Wadkins & C. Stadler
J.-M. Canizares & S. Torrance (4 & 3)	1	0	R. Floyd & B. Gilder
S. Ballesteros & P. Way	0	1	T. Kite & C. Peete (2 & 1)
FOURBALLS — AFTERNOON			
B. Waites & K. Brown (2 & 1)	1	0	G. Morgan & F. Zoeller
N. Faldo & B. Langer	0	1	T. Watson & J. Haas (2 & 1)
S. Ballesteros & P. Way (1 hole)	1	0	R. Floyd & C. Strange
S. Torrance & I. Woosnam (halved)	½	½	B. Crenshaw & C. Peete (halved)
FOURBALLS — MORNING			
B. Waites & K. Brown	0	1	L. Wadkins & C. Stadler (1 hole)
N. Faldo & B. Langer (4 & 2)	1	0	B. Crenshaw & C. Peete
S. Ballesteros & P. Way (halved)	½	½	G. Morgan & J. Haas (halved)
S. Torrance & I. Woosnam	0	1	T. Watson & B. Gilder (5 & 4)
FOURSOMES — AFTERNOON			
N. Faldo & B. Langer (3 & 2)	1	0	T. Kite & R. Floyd
S. Torrance & J.-M. Canizares	0	1	G. Morgan & L. Wadkins (7 & 5)
S. Ballesteros & P. Way (2 & 1)	1	0	T. Watson & B. Gilder
B. Waites & K. Brown	0	1	J. Haas & C. Strange (3 & 2)
SINGLES —			
S. Ballesteros (halved)	½	½	F. Zoeller (halved)
N. Faldo (2 & 1)	1	0	J. Haas
B. Langer (2 holes)	1	0	G. Morgan
G.J. Brand	0	1	B. Gilder (2 holes)
A. Lyle	0	1	B. Crenshaw (3 & 1)
B. Waites	0	1	C. Peete (1 hole)
P. Way (2 & 1)	1	0	C. Strange
S. Torrance (halved)	½	½	T. Kite (halved)
I. Woosnam	0	1	C. Stadler (3 & 2)
J.-M. Canizares (halved)	½	½	L. Wadkins (halved)
K. Brown (4 & 3)	1	0	R. Floyd
B. Gallacher	0	1	T. Watson (2 & 1)

13½   14½

VICTORIOUS CAPTAIN

JACK NICKLAUS (in 1981)

1985

The atmosphere at the Belfry leading up to the start of the 26th Ryder Cup was one of nervous expectation. Genuine optimism about Europe's chances had replaced the rather hopeful fantasies of previous years, as there was now hard evidence to suggest that the balance of power in golf was gradually shifting away from the Americans. There was a sense that the match at PGA National, far from being a one-off, had served notice that a new era in the tournament was about to begin. Even Jack Nicklaus had made Europe the favourites for the competition.

In the preceding months there had been much debate about the suitability of the Belfry as a venue. Gone were criticisms of it resembling 'a ploughed field' that had led to the Cup's relocation to Walton Heath in 1981, but in their place were concerns about whether it was the most suitable course on which to beat the Americans. Completed in 1975, the Belfry's design took its inspiration from the American style of golf course – namely 'target golf', with narrow fairways, thick rough and water features dominating the layout (the Belfry has water on eight holes). As the Americans had to play this type of course weekly on the US Tour, it was felt that the British PGA was handing them a clear advantage. United States Captain Lee Trevino boasted, 'My guy's love this course! It's so

The European team: (back row l–r) Sam Torrance, Seve Ballesteros, Ken Brown, Nick Faldo, Sandy Lyle, Howard Clark, José-Maria Olazábal and Manuel Piñero; (front row l–r) Paul Way, Ian Woosnam, Tony Jacklin (Capt.), Bernhard Langer and José Rivero.

The United States team: (back row l–r) Lanny Wadkins, Fuzzy Zoeller, Calvin Peete, Mark O'Meara, Ray Floyd, Hal Sutton, Tom Kite and Curtis Strange; (front row l–r) Hubert Green, Craig Stadler, Lee Trevino (Capt.), Andy North and Peter Jacobsen.

Americanized. It's what they're used to – with water hazards to fire over, rather than bump-and-run golf we get at your Open.' Refusing to be drawn on the subject, Tony Jacklin kept referring the media to what Peter Oosterhuis had told him – that the course would 'drive the Americans nuts'.

For the first time in the history of Ryder Cup, Europe could call on the services of three Major championship winners: Bernhard Langer had won the Masters in the Spring, Sandy Lyle was the new Open Champion, and Seve Ballesteros already had four Majors under his belt. Jacklin's wild-card picks were Nick Faldo, Ken Brown and José Rivero. Paul Way, José-Maria Canizares, Ian Woosnam, Sam Torrance, Manuel Piñero and Howard Clark all made it in by virtue of their standing in the European Tour order of merit.

Although the US had made an amendment to its selection procedure, which now allowed reigning Major champions to be selected automatically, the team lacked the figureheads of the past. In 1985, the only American player with superstar quality was Tom Watson, and he did not qualify. However, in Floyd, Wadkins, Kite, Stadler and Zoeller, Trevino did have some extremely tough matchplayers. With the addition of Andy North, Mark O'Meara, Peter Jacobsen, Hal Sutton and Hubert Green to the team, the Americans posed a considerable threat.

At 8.15am on the first day, amid a charged atmosphere, the first foursomes match got underway. The opening European pairing delivered the perfect start.

110

Ballesteros and Piñero raced into a four-hole lead against O'Meara and Strange, but a par at the 7th and a birdie at the 8th put the Americans back in the touch. With the 9th hole halved, the players moved on to the par-four 10th, which developed something of a cult status at the Ryder Cup that year.

Measuring just 275yd, and with its green protected by water, the 10th offered up an eagle chance for players brave enough to go for the green off the tee. A small plaque beside the tee commemorated the shot Ballesteros had played in 1978, when he was the first professional to drive the green. The Spaniard wasn't going to turn the opportunity down this time either. With customary flourish, he swept the ball off the tee and high into the air. It thudded onto the green and the crowd went berserk. For the rest of week, galleries standing ten deep huddled around the green, waiting for balls to fall from the sky.

Ballesteros's boldness had paid off, as he and Piñero went back to three up. An American comeback came too late, and when the 17th was halved, the Spaniards had won 2 and 1. Making their way back to the clubhouse, the pair was cheered all the way up the 18th. Behind them, however, the matches were not going Europe's way, as America sealed three comfortable victories to lead 3–1 at lunch.

At lunchtime Jacklin switched things around. Out went two of his own picks, Faldo and Brown, as well as Open Champion Sandy Lyle. In came Way and Woosnam, and Canizares would partner Langer in the fourballs.

ABOVE LEFT: *Seve Ballesteros drives the short par-four 10th.*

ABOVE: *Seve Ballesteros and Manuel Piñero proved a formidable pairing winning 3 out of 4 matches.*

It was an unbearably tense afternoon, as all but one of the matches went to the final hole. Way and Woosnam took an early lead, going two up at the 6th against Zoeller and Green, and when Way took the conventional route to the 10th and secured a birdie the pair was three up. But almost immediately the Americans struck back with birdies at the 12th and 13th holes. After another birdie at the 16th the match was all square. Coming down the 18th, both European drives found the bunker – with the Americans lying safe on the fairway, the prospects weren't looking good. That was until Way played a wonder shot out of the bunker to within 10ft of the hole. The Americans could not get inside his ball and missed both their birdie attempts. Way, who had played beautifully that season, made no mistake with his putt. With the overall score now at 3–2, the match was back on. Ballesteros and Piñero replicated their good morning form and won 2 and 1 again, this time beating North and Jacobsen. Langer and Canizares shared a point with Stadler and Sutton, while Wadkins and Floyd closed out Torrance and Clark at the last to secure America's first full point of the afternoon. Jacklin's lunchtime changes had been vindicated, as the new pairings collected 1½ points. The deficit was cut to just one point, with Europe trailing 3½–4½.

For all the golf played on day two – the hundreds of minutes the players spent out on the course battling away with one another – it would be one brief moment on the 18th green that was, and still is, remembered most. With two points to the American's one in the first three morning fourballs, Europe had levelled the scores at 5½ points each. Only the match between Lyle and Langer and Stadler and Strange was yet to be settled. It had been close for most of the round, with no more than one hole between the pairs. But when Stadler made birdie at the 13th it gave the Americans a two-hole cushion. Europe hit back immediately at the 14th, when Lyle made birdie. The 15th was halved, but when Strange put his approach to the 16th stone dead it left the Americans dormie – two up with two to play.

An eagle seemed the only probable way Europe could keep the match alive at the par-five 17th. Amazingly, Lyle delivered one, taking the match to the final hole. Strange bunkered his ball off the tee, and so it was left to Stadler to secure a par and a win. His second made it over the water and on to the green, but it ended up 25yd away from the hole. Lyle and Langer had both had birdie putts but both had missed, so Stadler needed to lag his first putt as close to the hole as possible, which he did. The ball drifted left on the slope, but not by much, and he left himself what appeared to be a simple tap-in. Now perhaps he

Sam Torrance and Howard Clark celebrate during their 2 and 1 victory over Tom Kite and Andy North on day two.

didn't hit it firmly enough, or imagined some borrow that wasn't there, but whatever happened Stadler struck his ball tamely and it drifted past the hole. To gasps of astonishment from the galleries, Stadler, hand on head, turned away and looked out across the lake in embarrassment and disbelief. Europe had claimed the most unlikely half point in Ryder Cup history.

Stadler's missed putt swung the momentum back to the Europeans, and they capitalized on it in the afternoon. Taking three out of four points, they now carried a 9–7 lead into the final day. Jacklin wasn't thinking about victory yet – at least not publicly – but the crowds certainly were, cheering the Europeans at every opportunity. There was the sense that a good start in the singles would carry the rest of the team over the winning line.

On the final day, Jacklin made a decision to put his best players in the middle of the singles draw, reasoning that if the early starters could get anything out of their games then the middle four of

ABOVE: *Craig Stadler turns away in dismay after missing an 18-inch putt to hand Europe an unlikely half point in the Saturday morning fourballs.*

FAR LEFT: *Ken Brown with his hickory-shafted putter.*

LEFT: *Bernhard Langer celebrates after sinking a putt during the Saturday afternoon foursomes against the United States pairing of Lanny Wadkins and Ray Floyd.*

Howard Clark, who narrowly missed a putt at the 17th to secure the point that would have won the Ryder Cup, completes victory over Mark O'Meara at the 18th.

Ballesteros, Lyle, Langer and Torrance could guide the team to victory. The first match out was between Piñero and Wadkins. Nobody expected the Spaniard to win, but having kept the match all square through the turn he then chipped in at the 10th to go one up. A par at the 11th was enough to go two up, and when he birdied the 15th he went three up. He could not lose. Wadkins clawed a hole back at the 16th, but a safe par-five at the 17th gave Piñero a win of 3 and 1. Europe was now three points ahead and needed only 4½ more to win the Ryder Cup.

The points were shared in the next two matches, Woosnam losing 2 and 1 to Stadler and Paul Way beating Ray Floyd by two holes. On the 18th fairway Floyd, needing birdie to halve the match, skimmed his ball into the lake, much to the delight of the partisan crowd. The score was Europe 11, USA 8. Now came the crucial four matches. Ballesteros nudged the total forward by half a point, and at almost the same time Lyle completed a win over Peter Jacobsen and Langer thrashed Hal Sutton 5 and 4. Suddenly the tension turned into celebration, as Europe needed just one point from the final six matches to win. With the team up in three of the matches, it only remained to find out who would have the honour of holing the winning putt.

Having sent a booming drive up the middle of the 18th fairway, Sam Torrance watched as his opponent Andy North drove the ball high and to the left into the lake. Barring a disaster, Torrance was going to win the hole and possibly the golden point that would take Europe to the crucial 14½ total.

Meanwhile, back on the 17th green, Howard Clark was a 6ft putt away from sealing the victory. But the ball lipped out and so it was time to rejoin Torrance for the historic finishing touch.

As Torrance made his way on to the fairway to find his perfect drive, he was met by Paul Way and Ian Woosnam, who confirmed that the Cup was indeed all but won. With tears in his eyes, Torrance sent his approach shot on its way, pitching the ball on to the green 20ft from the hole. Punching the air in delight, he walked up towards the green to a standing ovation. North, meanwhile, had played up on to the green in four and marked his ball. Torrance, with two putts for the hole, the match and the Ryder Cup, sent the ball on its way. It could not have been a more fitting moment. With near-perfect weight, the ball toppled into the hole. Arms aloft, an astonished Torrance looked over at his captain and shrugged as if to say 'We've done it'.

ABOVE LEFT: *Manuel Piñero, who got Europe off to such a positive start in the singles, beating Lanny Wadkins 3 and 1.*

ABOVE: *Arms aloft, Sam Torrance acknowledges the crowd after holing the putt that secures the Ryder Cup for Europe.*

LEFT: *The European team took to the Clubhouse roof to celebrate victory. Tony Jacklin acknowledges the cheers from the crowd.*

RIGHT: *Paul Way, Sam Torrance and Ian Woosnam enjoy the first of many champagne moments.*

BELOW: *The winning European team show off the Ryder Cup to British crowds for the first time in 28 years.*

The remaining matches played out to a finish, making the final score 16½–11½. Twenty-eight years after that heady afternoon at Lindrick, British and European golf had at last found some new heroes.

1985 THE BELFRY GOLF & COUNTRY CLUB, SUTTON COLDFIELD, WEST MIDLANDS

VICTORIOUS CAPTAIN

TONY JACKLIN

EUROPE			UNITED STATES
— FOURSOMES — MORNING			
S. Ballesteros & M. Piñero (2 & 1)	1	0	C. Strange & M. O'Meara
B. Langer & N. Faldo	0	1	C. Peete & T. Kite (3 & 2)
A. Lyle & K. Brown	0	1	L. Wadkins & R. Floyd (4 & 3)
H. Clark & S. Torrance	0	1	C. Stadler & H. Sutton (3 & 2)
— FOURBALLS — AFTERNOON			
P. Way & I. Woosnam (1 hole)	1	0	F. Zoeller & H. Green
S. Ballesteros & M. Piñero (2 & 1)	1	0	A. North & P. Jacobsen
B. Langer & J.-M. Canizares (halved)	½	½	C. Stadler & H. Sutton (halved)
S. Torrance & H. Clark	0	1	R. Floyd & L. Wadkins (1 hole)
— FOURBALLS — MORNING			
S. Torrance & H. Clark (2 & 1)	1	0	T. Kite & A. North
P. Way & I. Woosnam (4 & 3)	1	0	H. Green & F. Zoeller
S. Ballesteros & M. Piñero	0	1	M. O'Meara & L. Wadkins (3 & 2)
B. Langer & A. Lyle (halved)	½	½	C. Stadler & C. Strange (halved)
— FOURSOMES — AFTERNOON			
J.-M. Canizares & J. Rivero (4 & 3)	1	0	T. Kite & C. Peete
S. Ballesteros & M. Piñero (5 & 4)	1	0	C. Stadler & H. Sutton
P. Way & I. Woosnam	0	1	C. Strange & P. Jacobsen (4 & 2)
B. Langer & K. Brown (3 & 2)	1	0	R. Floyd & L. Wadkins
— SINGLES —			
M. Piñero (3 & 1)	1	0	L. Wadkins
I. Woosnam	0	1	C. Stadler (2 & 1)
P. Way (2 holes)	1	0	R. Floyd
S. Ballesteros (halved)	½	½	T. Kite (halved)
A. Lyle (3 & 2)	1	0	P. Jacobsen
B. Langer (5 & 4)	1	0	H. Sutton
S. Torrance (1 hole)	1	0	A. North
H. Clark (1 hole)	1	0	M. O'Meara
J. Rivero	0	1	C. Peete (1 hole)
N. Faldo	0	1	H. Green (3 & 1)
J.-M. Canizares (2 holes)	1	0	F. Zoeller
K. Brown	0	1	C. Strange (4 & 2)
16½			**11½**

The two captains, Tony Jacklin and Jack Nicklaus.

1987

It had now been 60 years since Ted Ray and his British team had stood on the deck of SS *Aquitania* at Southampton docks to pose for a historic photograph before they set sail for the United States. As the 14th European team boarded Concorde to fly to Columbus, Ohio, in September 1987, they did so in the knowledge that the match at Muirfield Village marked their best opportunity for a first victory on American soil. However, they would have to do it on 'the course that Jack built'.

Shortly after winning his first Open Championship at Muirfield in 1966, Jack Nicklaus bought a plot of land near his hometown of Columbus and slowly transformed it into Muirfield Village. His creation produced some giddy praise. 'Here is truly a sporting Garden of Eden,' *The Times* reported, 'simultaneously voluptuous and sinister.' The greens were 'set like banqueting tables, surrounded by quicksand' and, so claimed the greenkeeper, were faster than a pool table. Muirfield was, according to some, 'the Augusta of the North' and made a fitting memorial to Nicklaus's spectacular career.

In a further attempt to overawe their European visitors, the USPGA appointed Jack Nicklaus as captain for the second time. With Jacklin as European captain for the third time, it would be the sixth occasion the two had met in the Ryder Cup. For Jacklin there were further landmarks to celebrate, as it was now 20 years since he had made his debut. If the Champions Club in Houston had been the nadir of his and Europe's Cup experience, Muirfield Village presented an opportunity to create history of a more positive nature.

The main talking point leading up to the match was the relative strength of the two teams. The Europeans had the best players (Ballesteros, Langer, Faldo and Lyle) but the United States had greater strength in terms of depth, with all 12 of the players in the top 40 of the world rankings, compared to just six from Europe. The result at the Belfry had, to say the very least, ruffled a few American feathers and led people to question the Americans' claim that they still had the best golfers. All the talk of shifts in power got some of their players hot under the collar. Lanny Wadkins launched a vociferous attack on what he thought were the inflated reputations of some of Europe's golfers: 'I get sick and tired of reading all that stuff about Ballesteros and Langer being the best', he said before the match. 'If they are the best then why haven't they won in

America in two years?' And Payne Stewart confirmed the team's sensitivity when he stated, 'We've got the best tour in the world and we've got the best players.' In truth, this was all a bit of gamesmanship, because the Americans knew that that there wasn't much difference between the sides. The winner would be the team that could handle the pressure best.

The European side included nine members of the triumphant Belfry team, blooded two new players (José-Maria Olazábal and Gordon Brand Jr) and welcomed back an old face from the past, Irishman Eamonn Darcy. The Americans had five debutants – Larry Mize (fresh from his chip-in at the Masters), Dan Pohl, Mark Calcavecchia, Payne Stewart and Scott Simpson – who would blend with the experience of Ben Crenshaw and Larry Nelson, plus four of the players who had lost in 1985.

By the middle of the first morning on the opening day, it appeared that the pre-match comments made by Lanny Wadkins and Payne Stewart had been well judged after all. The Americans raced into a lead in all four matches and by midday had already won the first two. But Europe clawed back, taking the

last two matches to claim a psychological advantage as they went into the afternoon fourballs. Faldo and Woosnam turned a four-hole deficit at the 9th into a two-hole victory at the 18th, leaving Wadkins unamused. The first outing for the pairing of Ballesteros and Olazábal also secured a victory on the last hole after having been two down at the 6th.

The momentum of these victories propelled the European players to a clean sweep of the afternoon fourballs, something they had never achieved in all the 26 previous Cup encounters. American claims about Europe's lack of strength in depth now looked rather misjudged.

In a confident step, Jacklin had sent rookie Brand Jr out with Rivero first to face Crenshaw and Simpson. Four birdies in ten holes produced a four-hole lead that they didn't relinquish. Langer and Lyle then fought back from being two down with five to play to win by one hole. When Faldo/Woosnam and Ballesteros/Olazábal both completed their second victories of the day, the match score stood at Europe 6, USA 2.

If Lanny Wadkins needed any proof of what a good player Bernhard Langer was, he got it on the second day. Paired with Larry Nelson, Wadkins watched Langer and Lyle shade a close match 2 and 1 in the morning foursomes. Faldo and Woosnam could only manage a half, after looking like they might win their match against Sutton and Mize. But the Europeans stretched their lead to five points when Olazábal holed out from 7ft on the 18th green to give himself and Ballesteros a deserved one-hole victory against Crenshaw and Stewart.

In the afternoon fourballs, Faldo and Woosnam stretched Europe's lead further with a comfortable 5 and 4 victory over Strange and Kite, before the Americans struck back twice to reduce the deficit. So it was left to Langer and Lyle to try to hold off Wadkins and Nelson and put overall victory in sight.

The Europeans had control of the match and were dormie three standing on the 16th tee. Then back came Wadkins, winning that hole and the 17th with birdies, to put Europe's point in doubt. But in the fading light the European pair slammed the door shut on the Americans. Lyle was first to play and put his ball to within 5ft of the hole. Langer stepped up next, eight-iron in hand, to hit the shot of the match, his ball almost landing in the hole and coming to rest 6in from the cup. For an emotional Jacklin, words were hard to find. His pairings had worked better than he could ever have imagined and Europe was nearly there.

The 2,000-strong European support crowd would have to wait a few hours before they could celebrate on the final day. Woosnam lost the opening singles match to Andy Bean by one hole, while Howard Clark beat Dan Pohl by the same margin. Torrance scrapped with Larry Mize to share a point, leaving a further two to be found from the remaining nine matches. A run of four American victories – Calcavecchia, Stewart, Simpson and Kite – did not settle the nerves and took the hosts to within one point of Europe. But then along came Eamonn Darcy.

Drawn against Ben Crenshaw, Darcy was helped on his way when the Texan, having just missed a putt to lose the 6th hole, slammed his putter against the ground, snapping it in two. Unable to fix it, Crenshaw spent the rest of the round putting with his one-iron. Darcy promptly went three up, but back came Crenshaw. Amazingly, the American went ahead at the 16th, only to see Darcy square the match at the next. Crenshaw's nerves surfaced first on the 18th, when his drive found trouble and he took a further four shots to get down. A bogey five resulted. Having put his approach in the bunker, Darcy recovered to leave himself a 4ft putt, for the hole and the match. However, it was a perilously fast downhill putt, which if it had missed the hole may well have slid past it by 5–10ft. He gathered himself together and feathered the ball with his putter, letting the ball's weight carry it towards the hole. An agonizing two seconds later the ball disappeared. He'd done it.

Somehow it seems appropriate that Eamonn Darcy should be the man who people remember most from the last day. His first appearance had been at Laurel Valley, when Britain and Ireland were still bogged down in the mire of the 1970s. Darcy's final-day win (his first in 11 attempts), which left Europe on the brink of victory, ensured that his idiosyncratic swing would be the second thing that people remembered about him.

At precisely 2.50pm Europe retained the Ryder Cup. Appropriately enough, it was Seve Ballesteros, the man Jacklin had built his team around, who delivered the historic point, holing out on the 17th green to beat Curtis Strange 2 and 1. Bernhard Langer and Gordon Brand Jr secured halves to claim outright victory, making the final score Europe 15, USA 13. The celebrations could begin.

Jacklin spent the next hours brushing back tears from the corner of his eyes. 'It's the greatest week of my life,' he said. His players hoisted him up on their

THE 1980s

RIGHT: *Tony Jacklin and Seve Ballesteros were at the heart of Europe's success in the 1980s.*

BELOW: *The victorious European team hold court on the 18th green at Muirfield Village.*

shoulders, whilst Olazábal jigged around on the 18th green. Jacklin had achieved what no previous British or European captain had done and beaten the Americans in their own backyard.

1987 MUIRFIELD VILLAGE, COLUMBUS, OHIO

	EUROPE		UNITED STATES
— FOURSOMES — MORNING			
S. Torrance & H. Clark	0	1	C. Strange & T. Kite (4 & 2)
K. Brown & B. Langer	0	1	H. Sutton & D. Pohl (2 & 1)
N. Faldo & I. Woosnam (2 holes)	1	0	L. Wadkins & L. Mize
S. Ballesteros & J.-M. Olazábal (1 hole)	1	0	L. Nelson & P. Stewart
— FOURBALLS — AFTERNOON			
G. Brand Jr & J. Rivero (3 & 2)	1	0	B. Crenshaw & S. Simpson
A. Lyle & B. Langer (1 hole)	1	0	A. Bean & M. Calcavecchia
N. Faldo & I. Woosnam (2 & 1)	1	0	H. Sutton & D. Pohl
S. Ballesteros & J.-M. Olazábal (2 & 1)	1	0	C. Strange & T. Kite
— FOURBALLS — MORNING			
J. Rivero & G. Brand Jr	0	1	C. Strange & T. Kite (3 & 1)
N. Faldo & I. Woosnam (halved)	½	½	H. Sutton & L. Mize (halved)
A. Lyle & B. Langer (2 & 1)	1	0	L. Wadkins & L. Nelson
S. Ballesteros & J.-M. Olazábal (1 hole)	1	0	B. Crenshaw & P. Stewart
— FOURSOMES — AFTERNOON			
N. Faldo & I. Woosnam (5 & 4)	1	0	C. Strange & T. Kite
E. Darcy & G. Brand Jr	0	1	A. Bean & P. Stewart (3 & 2)
S. Ballesteros & J.-M. Olazábal	0	1	H. Sutton & L. Mize (2 & 1)
S. Lyle & B. Langer (1 hole)	1	0	L. Wadkins & L. Nelson
— SINGLES —			
I. Woosnam	0	1	A. Bean (1 hole)
H. Clark (1 hole)	1	0	D. Pohl
S. Torrance (halved)	½	½	L. Mize (halved)
N. Faldo	0	1	M. Calcavecchia (1 hole)
J.-M. Olazábal	0	1	P. Stewart (2 holes)
J. Rivero	0	1	S. Simpson (2 & 1)
A. Lyle	0	1	T. Kite (3 & 2)
E. Darcy (1 hole)	1	0	B. Crenshaw
B. Langer (halved)	½	½	L. Nelson (halved)
S. Ballesteros (2 & 1)	1	0	C. Strange
K. Brown	0	1	L. Wadkins (3 & 2)
G. Brand Jr (halved)	½	½	H. Sutton (halved)

VICTORIOUS CAPTAIN
TONY JACKLIN

15   13

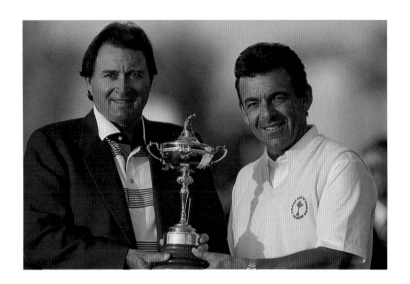

The two captains, Raymond Floyd and Tony Jacklin.

1989

The last match of the 1980s would also signal the end of Tony Jacklin's reign as European captain. What had started with personal rejection, when he was left out of the team at Walton Heath, had ended with universal admiration. In the space of eight years he had taken Europe from being no-hopers to the favourites to retain the trophy at the Belfry in 1989. And having achieved the impossible by beating the US on the course that Jack built, it appeared now that anything was possible. But the Europeans were to face an American team that was determined not to lose for a third time in succession.

Raymond Floyd's career had already spanned three decades when he was elected captain of the US team that would play at the Belfry. Having always been a gutsy and patriotic player, he placed high value on winning the Ryder Cup back, but not at all costs. Before the match Floyd had made a point of impressing upon his players the importance of sportsmanship, etiquette and camaraderie when competing. These were noble sentiments, which made his comments at the pre-match banquet all the more bizarre. Floyd introduced his team as 'the 12 best players in the world'. In trying to imitate Ben Hogan's 1967 speech, he had not only got it spectacularly wrong but had incensed the European team as well. As if to highlight the ridiculousness of the remark, Tony Jacklin was encouraged, but declined, to introduce Seve Ballesteros as 'the 13th best player in the world'. It was perfectly acceptable for someone like Hogan to boast when the US team hadn't lost once in 30 years, but coming off the back of two defeats Floyd's claim sounded hollow and misjudged.

In the wake of the American defeat at Muirfield Village, Jack Nicklaus had argued that the European Tour was more competitive than the US Tour. Europe was producing players that were more used to winning tournaments and this had given them the edge on the final day. 'Winning is winning', Nicklaus said. 'It doesn't matter if it's the Hong Kong fourball. The Europeans are more used to it than we are'. The Belfry team had a familiar look about it, with eight players from the team that had won in 1987. Four new members joined them: Europe's leading money-winner, Ronan Rafferty, who made his first appearance; 41-year-old Christy O'Connor, who reappeared after a 14-year gap (how things had changed since he last played in a Ryder Cup!); and returnees José-Maria Canizares and Mark James.

For some of the American team, their newfound acquaintance with losing matches was becoming difficult to stomach. This seemed true in particular for Mark Calcavecchia, who recalled how he had felt after the 1987 defeat: 'All I can remember were the grins on their [the Europeans'] faces. If you ask me it was sickening that they won and we didn't.'

Of the other nine players who qualified for the US team, only Tom Kite and Curtis Strange were experienced Ryder Cup campaigners. With this in mind, Floyd picked Tom Watson and Lanny Wadkins to bolster what was a young team – a decision he was criticized for, as Wadkins in particular had had a poor season. Along with Calcavecchia, Payne Stewart and Mark O'Meara, five debutants – Paul Azinger, Chip Beck, Mark McCumber, Ken Green and Fred Couples – would complete the team.

On the first morning the Americans raced into a 3–1 lead, as they had done four years earlier. Tom Kite and Curtis Strange earned a half point with the star pairing of Faldo and Woosnam, while Wadkins and Stewart beat Clark and James at the last hole. A half for Watson and Beck must have felt like a whole point against the virtually unbeatable Ballesteros and Olazábal, and Calcavecchia and Green beat Langer and Rafferty 2 and 1.

The afternoon could not have been more different for the European players, as they made a clean sweep of the points in the fourballs. Ballesteros and Olazábal won 6 and 5 against Watson and O'Meara, and Faldo and Woosnam were two-hole winners over Calcavecchia and McCumber. In their first outing as a pair, Sam Torrance and Gordon Brand Jr overcame Strange and Azinger by one hole. Brand Jr, who was playing his first Ryder Cup in Britain, was astonished by the level of support: 'The spectators were clapping us all the way. You feel two up before you start.'

On the second morning the points were shared, but only just. Ballesteros and Olazábal had been three up at one stage during their match with Kite and Strange, but the Americans had fought back over the closing holes and began the 18th knowing they had to win the hole to halve the match. Ballesteros had put his partner in a greenside bunker and the Americans missed a chance for birdie, but they still looked odds-on to win the hole. Olazábal played a wonderful bunker shot and left Ballesteros a simple tap-in to secure the point.

Nick Faldo points out the line of a putt to his playing partner Ian Woosnam during their second-day foursomes match against Lanny Watkins and Payne Stewart.

In the afternoon fourballs the Americans had taken two points from the first two games with safe, if not comfortable, 2 and 1 wins. The third match was looking as though it would go the same way. Mark James and Howard Clark had kept in touch with Payne Stewart and Curtis Strange, but they could never establish parity with them. With four holes to play, the two Yorkshiremen were one down. Against the run of play, the Europeans conjured up two birdies on the 16th and 17th and turned the match on its head to go one up. With the marathon 474yd 18th to come, it looked as though a par four would be enough. Off the tee, Clark's ball landed 6in over the lake. James then struck a glorious three-iron on to the green and made par. The Americans could not compete with this, and from being favourites for the match on the 16th tee, they had lost by one. Mind you, they hadn't so much lost the point as had it snatched from their grasp by some heroic play. Tony Jacklin was ecstatic. With Ballesteros and Olazábal winning their match moments earlier on the 16th green – making it 3½ points out of a possible four for the Spaniards – the European team took exactly the same lead (9–7) into the singles as they had done four years earlier.

As daylight broke and the course was basked in sunlight, the memory of that glorious Sunday four years before was easy to recall: the crowds chanting and cheering as Sam Torrance raised his putter to the sky as if to salute them, the celebrations on the clubhouse roof, champagne everywhere, Concorde flying past… But this would be a different day, with new dramas to script and new heroes to anoint.

For the Americans, a singles result equal to the one they had achieved at Muirfield Village (7½–4½) would be enough for them to reclaim the Ryder Cup. And even though they trailed 9–7, their history of dominance on the final day suggested that the match was evenly poised.

Jacklin split his best players up, putting Ballesteros, Langer and Olazábal in the top three singles matches. At the bottom, Faldo and Woosnam would hopefully see Europe through should the match go down to the wire. But things did not go to plan.

The two-point lead that Europe had taken into the final day was wiped out before the top match between Ballesteros and Azinger had even finished. Tom Kite had beaten Howard Clark by a staggering 8 and 7, while Chip Beck beat Bernhard Langer 3 and 2. And this was before the heartbreak that Ballesteros was about to suffer on the 18th. The Spaniard needed to win the final hole to salvage half a point against Azinger, and when the American drove his ball into

Tom Watson chips onto the green in the opening day foursomes.

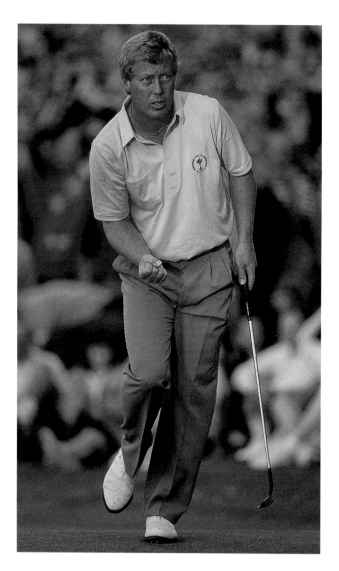

the water, it looked odds-on that he would. But playing his second from the semi-rough, Ballesteros dumped his ball in the water short of the green. Azinger, meanwhile, had put his third shot into the bunker left of the green. Ballesteros put his second ball on the green and left himself a long putt for a bogey, which he made. But Azinger, an acknowledged master out of the sand, got up and down and secured a point.

With the overall points now standing at Europe 9, USA 10, an increasingly anxious crowd scanned the scoreboards hoping to find some comfort in the matches still being played. Soon enough, Olazábal and Rafferty both provided one-hole wins, and with cheers ringing out around the 16th green, the scoreboard confirmed that Mark James had beaten Mark O'Meara 3 and 2. Suddenly, it was Europe 12, USA 10.

Europe was in touching distance of retaining the Cup when up stepped the two oldest men on the course to provide the finale. Christy O'Connor Jr had been

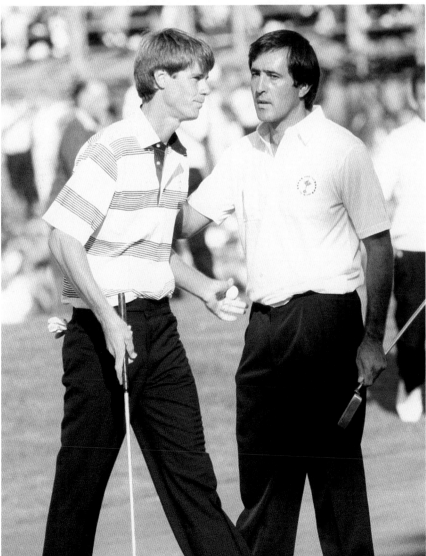

ABOVE: *Seve Ballesteros hits his approach to the 18th green into the water.*

LEFT: *Seve Ballesteros congratulates Paul Azinger on his one-hole victory in the opening singles match.*

trailing Fred Couples until the 16th hole, where he fired a wedge to 3ft, holed the birdie putt and squared the match. With the 17th squared, it was off down the last. Couples hit one of the longest drives of the week at the 18th. O'Connor followed him down the fairway but was 60–70yd behind, then with 200yd to the flag he struck a two-iron. Low and straight it flew over the water, landing on the green and rolling up to within 4ft of the hole. It was quite the most magnificent shot. Under pressure, Couples pushed his approach wide and to the right and then chipped poorly. With a five being the best he could do, he walked up to O'Connor and conceded the match. The crowd was

ABOVE: *Christy O'Connor Jr offers up a prayer of thanks after defeating Fred Couples by one. O'Connor's two-iron approach to the 18th was the shot of the 28th Ryder Cup.*

RIGHT: *José-Maria Canizares does a jig on the 18th green after holing the putt that retained the Ryder Cup.*

OPPOSITE PAGE

TOP: *Tony Jacklin hugs the Ryder Cup in his final match as European captain.*

BOTTOM: *Europe celebrates retaining the Ryder Cup.*

in raptures as O'Connor looked skywards and offered up a small prayer of thanks. He had just added to his family's rich heritage in the Ryder Cup.

Ten minutes later, Europe secured the vital point that retained the trophy. Canizares came down the last all square in his match with Ken Green. Both men hit the green but didn't threaten the hole. Canizares putted down the green, leaving himself 3ft for par, but Green raced his ball 6ft past. While Green missed the return putt, Canizares made his. Tony Jacklin had become the first captain in the history of the Ryder Cup to carry off the trophy three times in succession.

But it wasn't quite over. The score read Europe 14, USA 10, and with four matches out on the course the Americans could still tie the match. Astonishingly, they did just that. McCumber, Watson, Wadkins and Strange all won, Strange's long iron to the final green being the equal of O'Connor's earlier on in the afternoon.

It had been an enthralling contest, which, despite a bad start, had been notable for the sportsmanship that both teams showed. Captain Jacklin had bowed out in style.

1989 THE BELFRY GOLF & COUNTRY CLUB, SUTTON COLDFIELD, WEST MIDLANDS

EUROPE			UNITED STATES
— FOURSOMES — MORNING			
N. Faldo & I. Woosnam (halved)	½	½	T. Kite & C. Strange (halved)
H. Clark & M. James	0	1	L. Wadkins & P. Stewart (1 hole)
S. Ballesteros & J.-M. Olazábal (halved)	½	½	T. Watson & C. Beck (halved)
B. Langer & R. Rafferty	0	1	M. Calcavecchia & K. Green (2 & 1)
— FOURBALLS — AFTERNOON			
S. Torrance & G. Brand Jr (1 hole)	1	0	C. Strange & P. Azinger
H. Clark & M. James (3 & 2)	1	0	F. Couples & L. Wadkins
N. Faldo & I. Woosnam (2 holes)	1	0	M. Calcavecchia & M. McCumber
S. Ballesteros & J.-M. Olazábal (6 & 5)	1	0	T. Watson & M. O'Meara
— FOURBALLS — MORNING			
I. Woosnam & N. Faldo (3 & 2)	1	0	L. Wadkins & P. Stewart
G. Brand Jr & S. Torrance	0	1	C. Beck & P. Azinger (4 & 3)
C. O'Connor Jr & R. Rafferty	0	1	M. Calcavecchia & K. Green (3 & 2)
S. Ballesteros & J.-M. Olazábal (1 hole)	1	0	T. Kite & C. Strange
— FOURSOMES — AFTERNOON			
N. Faldo & I. Woosnam	0	1	C. Beck & P. Azinger (2 & 1)
B. Langer & J.-M. Canizares	0	1	T. Kite & M. McCumber (2 & 1)
H. Clark & M. James (1 hole)	1	0	P. Stewart & C. Strange
S. Ballesteros & J.-M. Olazábal (4 & 2)	1	0	M. Calcavecchia & K. Green
— SINGLES —			
S. Ballesteros	0	1	P. Azinger (1 hole)
B. Langer	0	1	C. Beck (3 & 2)
J.-M. Olazábal (1 hole)	1	0	P. Stewart
R. Rafferty (1 hole)	1	0	M. Calcavecchia
H. Clark	0	1	T. Kite (8 & 7)
M. James (3 & 2)	1	0	M. O'Meara
C. O'Connor Jr (1 hole)	1	0	F. Couples
J.-M. Canizares (1 hole)	1	0	K. Green
G. Brand Jr	0	1	M. McCumber (1 hole)
S. Torrance	0	1	T. Watson (3 & 1)
N. Faldo	0	1	L. Wadkins (1 hole)
I. Woosnam	0	1	C. Strange (2 holes)

VICTORIOUS CAPTAIN

TONY JACKLIN

14   14

THE 1990s

1991–1999

1991

In a decade that would be noted for its epic confrontations, the match at the Ocean Course on Kiawah Island was by far the most dramatic. Its climax would live up to the pre-match hype, when the fate of the Cup was decided by the last putt on the 18th green in the final singles match. The contest was played against a backdrop of intense American patriotism following the Gulf War campaign, and as a consequence it was always going to be a supercharged affair. And having lost the last three matches, the United States didn't need an excuse to get pumped up. During the build-up to the tournament, it was billed as 'the War on the Shore', and from thereon in so it was known. It's not actually clear whether the 'war' part was ever that appropriate, but the 'shore' certainly was.

The two captains, Bernard Gallacher and Dave Stockton.

Newly opened in 1991, the Ocean Course was carved out of a 3-mile stretch of coastal dune in South Carolina, with views looking out on to the Atlantic. Measuring just over 7,300yd, the course was described by Sam Torrance after he'd played his first practice round on it as 'an absolute monster'. It didn't have any bunkers, just vast stretches of sand and grit flanking the fairways, and if the sand didn't catch your ball, a swamp or even an alligator might. It was a difficult course even without the wind constantly blowing in off the Atlantic.

The drama started – as was becoming the norm – even before the matches got underway. While travelling to the opening gala dinner, Steve Pate – the top-rated US player coming into the event – was involved in a car crash. He sustained bruising to his ribs, which meant that he would play almost no part in the contest.

The European players, meanwhile, had arrived safely, but they hadn't been getting much sleep. A North Carolina disc jockey had broadcast the telephone number of the European team's hotel and had then encouraged his listeners to 'wake up the enemy' by telephoning the players in the middle of the night. Small-minded pranks aside, new captain Bernard Gallacher had cause to feel confident about his team's prospects. Along with the top three ranked players in the world – Ian Woosnam, José-Maria Olazábal and Nick Faldo – the Europeans had Ballesteros, Langer, James and Torrance all on board. Between them, the players had 32 Ryder Cup appearances. The weight of this experience was counterbalanced by the presence of five rookies: David Feherty, Steven Richardson, David Gilford, Paul Broadhurst and Colin Montgomerie.

With Pate injured just hours before the first matches, it was too late to call in a replacement and US captain Dave Stockton had to make do with the 11 fit players he already had. Seven had played in the drawn match at the Belfry, and Ray Floyd switched from his duties as the previous captain to play in his seventh Ryder Cup at the age of 49. Hale Irwin, who had been enjoying a renaissance, came back on to the team after ten years, while Corey Pavin and Wayne Levi made their debuts.

It was a case of groundhog morning for the Europeans on the first day. For the third time in four attempts, the United States won the opening foursomes by three matches to one. Only Ballesteros and Olazábal managed a point, in what was a controversial game with Azinger and Beck.

The problems started at the 7th hole. Chip Beck had teed off at the 7th with a ball of different compression to the one he had started with at the 1st, and that contravened the one-ball rule. But the Americans had escaped a penalty because Ballesteros and Olazábal only brought the matter up on the 9th green (the rule stipulates that an objection has to be submitted to the referee before the players tee off at the next hole). Olazábal had not been aware of the need to bring the issue up immediately and had consequently sent for Bernard Gallacher to seek his advice on the matter. Players and officials convened on the 10th tee and

José-Maria Olazábal looks on as Seve Ballesteros drives on the 4th hole at the Ocean Course, during their controversial foursomes match with Paul Azinger and Chip Beck, which Europe won 2 and 1.

The patriotic American crowds at Kiawah Island in a quieter moment.

spent the next ten minutes discussing the matter. Azinger had admitted to using the wrong ball, but questioned why the issue hadn't been brought up immediately. As the American pair had just gone three up, they naturally thought – with some justification – that this was gamesmanship on the part of the Spaniards. A heated discussion between the players ended when the referee, who had no option, ruled in favour of the Americans, and the match continued.

Whatever the rights and wrongs, the match changed course dramatically from thereon in. A three-putt by the Americans on the 10th green brought the match back to two up, followed by a gorgeous second shot to the 12th by Olazábal that left a tap-in for Ballesteros – one up. And then on the 13th Ballesteros holed a 6-footer to bring the match back to all square. Europe took the lead on the 15th, when Olazábal put a recovery shot stone dead, and when Ballesteros holed a 25ft putt on the 17th the match was won 2 and 1. A five-hole swing in eight holes had given Europe its first point.

The Europeans fought back further in the afternoon fourballs. David Ferherty was partnering his old friend Sam Torrance, and had spent the morning in a permanent state of fear at the prospect of playing his first Ryder Cup match. After he scuffed his putt on the first green, leaving it short and wide, Torrance took him to one side and said: 'If you don't pull yourself together, I'm going to join them [Wadkins and O'Meara], and you can play all three of us, you useless bastard!' It did the trick. On the 11th Ferherty chipped in, at the 14th he holed a 5ft putt and on the 18th his 10ft putt earned the pair a valuable half.

Ballesteros and Olazábal discuss the line of a putt. The Spanish pair were the most successful pairing in Ryder Cup history, losing only twice in 15 matches.

Ballesteros and Olazábal drew Azinger and Beck again in the afternoon and this time beat them without controversy by the same margin. Richardson made a wonderful start to his Ryder Cup career, holing a 25ft putt on the 6th and chipping in for an eagle at the next. He and his partner, Mark James, completed a convincing 5 and 4 win over Pavin and Calcavecchia. In contrast to these successes, the previously formidable pairing of Woosnam and Faldo suffered their second loss of the day, going down 5 and 3 to Floyd and Couples. The score stood at 4½–3½ to the United States at the end of the first day.

As Faldo and Woosnam did not seem to be clicking, Gallacher decided to rest Woosnam in the morning of the second day and pair Faldo with new boy David Gilford. However, it proved to be a poor combination. Faldo, as was his wont sometimes, appeared to be in a world of his own and rarely communicated with Gilford. Between them they conspired to crash to a 7 and 6 defeat to Azinger and O'Meara. This gave the Americans their third point of the morning. It was only Ballesteros and Olazábal who stopped the foursomes becoming a clean sweep for the United States, beating Floyd and Couples 3 and 2.

Gallacher had to make changes at lunchtime or the match would drift away from Europe. He gambled on some new pairings, bringing back Woosnam to partner Broadhurst, joining Montgomerie with Langer, and allowing James to provide the experience in his pairing with Richardson. The changes worked perfectly, delivering three points. For once, however, Ballesteros and Olazábal managed only a half. Even so, the Europeans had dragged themselves back into the match, to level the scores at 8–8. Would it be enough though? After all, in 28 tournaments the Americans had lost the singles only four times.

News broke early on the third day that Steve Pate had not recovered sufficiently from his injuries to play in the singles, which meant that Bernard Gallacher had to nominate a European player to sit them out. David Gilford was the unlucky man. He'd had a pretty miserable two days already and it was unfortunate that he wasn't given the chance to put things right on the last day. However, his chance would come in the future. With the teams sharing the point of the cancelled match, the scores now stood at 8½ points each.

The Europeans got off to their best start in eight years, taking 2½ points from the opening three matches. Faldo had been sent out first against Floyd and immediately forged an advantage, going three up in as many holes. He improved that by one at the 11th and appeared to be in control. But Floyd won the next hole and the 14th to make the outcome less certain. Faldo then regrouped and with a par at the 18th secured a two-hole win.

Moments earlier, Ferherty had steadied his nerves enough to beat Payne Stewart 2 and 1 at the 17th. Mark Calcavecchia imploded in his match with Colin Montgomerie. The American was four up with four to play, but then gifted Montgomerie a half by dropping seven strokes in the remaining holes. Arriving at the long par-three 17th, the Scot failed to carry the water off the tee. Anywhere on dry land would have done for Calcavecchia, but he played a horrid low slice that skimmed into the water. He then took three putts for a six and Montgomerie won the hole with a double-bogey five. A four at the last was enough to give Europe an unlikely half.

The Americans responded with three wins in the next four matches. On completing his two-hole victory over Olazábal, Azinger, clearly pumped up, punched the air and gestured to the spectators to make more noise, which they dutifully did. Back on the 17th, Corey 'Crazy' Pavin was whipping up the crowds

BELOW LEFT: *Paul Azinger punches the air in celebration as he holes a putt.*

BELOW: *Corey Pavin wills his ball on towards the hole at the 17th during his singles match with Steven Richardson.*

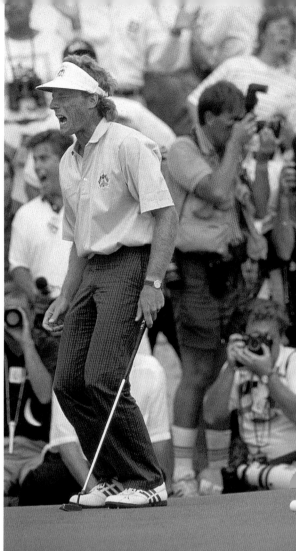

into even more of a frenzy as he played out of a bunker. On finishing his stroke, he leapt out of the trap and ran halfway across the green to wave theatrically and will his ball towards the hole. The shot, which finished 18in from the hole, secured him a 2 and 1 victory over Richardson. With Chip Beck completing a disappointing Cup for Woosnam, beating him 3 and 1, it was left to Ballesteros to keep the European score ticking along with a win over Wayne Levi.

The score was 12–12, with four matches left on the course, although European prospects were looking gloomy as America was ahead in three of these. Paul Broadhurst delivered a point for Europe, but then Couples and Wadkins both won to take the American total to 14 points. They could not lose.

With all the excitement of the other matches, not much attention had been paid to the final pairing of Langer and Irwin. It was probably thought that the Cup would be decided before they finished their match. But as the afternoon wore on and results came in, it became clear that this was going to be the pivotal game. Langer had spent most of the match trying to prise a two-hole lead away from Irwin, then at the 15th his persistence finally paid off. A brave 6ft putt took him back to one down. At the 17th, Irwin three-putted, leaving them all square going down the last. Suddenly, they were the only show in town. Large crowds that had been scattered around the course all converged at the 18th hole. Langer hit a solid drive and found the fairway, while Irwin pulled his ball left into the thick stuff, only for it to reappear miraculously on the fairway some moments later. Irwin, whose nerve had spectacularly deserted him, missed the green with his approach, but Langer, ever the cool customer, safely found it, 30ft away from the hole. Irwin then made a mess of his chip, leaving his ball 25ft away in three. Advantage Europe. After much deliberation, Langer sent his putt towards the hole, hoping to lag it close. But the ball drifted left and came to rest 6ft away. Irwin somehow managed to putt his ball to within 2ft of the hole and Langer generously conceded the putt. The German now had a putt to win his match and tie the scores at 14–14.

In the gathering gloom, Langer began to line up his putt. Back and forth he walked, and then to the side and back again, looking for the definitive proof of the line he should take. He made a lingering inspection of the spike marks around the hole, which, given the situation, must have looked like huge scars in the turf. The crowds squeezed in closer to the green, a few whispers floated around the galleries and then there was silence. Langer was ready to putt. He settled over the ball, gripped his putter, paused, then let it go. The putt looked good, but as the ball slowed, it drifted to the right, touching the hole on its way past. As it did, Langer's knees buckled and he screamed in anguish. Europe had lost the Ryder Cup, 14½–13½.

The American team was both elated and relieved. Some of the crowd didn't behave themselves, having cheered when Langer missed his putt. But the American players were mostly gracious in victory. Even so, they did have their moments, with Paul Azinger winning the prize for the most ridiculous quote of the week: 'American pride is back. We went over there and thumped the Iraqis. Now we've taken the Cup back. I'm proud to be an American.'

It wasn't long before the inevitable chants of 'U-S-A' came spilling out

The winning United States team: (back row l–r) Lanny Wadkins, Fred Couples, Paul Azinger, Ray Floyd, Hale Irwin, Dave Stockton (Capt.), Payne Stewart and Mark Calcavecchia; (front row l–r) Chip Beck, Mark O'Meara, Steve Pate, Corey Pavin and Wayne Levi.

from sections of the crowd. The European team must have looked out across the Atlantic and longed for home. Kiawah had been extreme in every sense – the build-up, the matches, the course, the crowds and the final torturous act.

1991 OCEAN COURSE, KIAWAH ISLAND, SOUTH CAROLINA

EUROPE			UNITED STATES
— *FOURSOMES* — MORNING			
S. Ballesteros & J.-M. Olazábal (2 & 1)	1	0	P. Azinger & C. Beck
B. Langer & M. James	0	1	R. Floyd & F. Couples (2 & 1)
D. Gilford & C. Montgomerie	0	1	L. Wadkins & H. Irwin (4 & 2)
N. Faldo & I. Woosnam	0	1	P. Stewart & M. Calcavecchia (1 hole)
— *FOURBALLS* — AFTERNOON			
S. Torrance & D. Feherty (halved)	½	½	L. Wadkins & M. O'Meara (halved)
S. Ballesteros & J.-M. Olazábal (2 & 1)	1	0	P. Azinger & C. Beck
S. Richardson & M. James (5 & 4)	1	0	C. Pavin & M. Calcavecchia
N. Faldo & I. Woosnam	0	1	R. Floyd & F. Couples (5 & 3)
— *FOURSOMES* — MORNING			
D. Feherty & S. Torrance	0	1	H. Irwin & L. Wadkins (4 & 2)
M. James & S. Richardson	0	1	M. Calcavecchia & P. Stewart (1 hole)
N. Faldo & D. Gilford	0	1	P. Azinger & M. O'Meara (7 & 6)
S. Ballesteros & J.-M. Olazábal (3 & 2)	1	0	F. Couples & R. Floyd
— *FOURBALLS* — AFTERNOON			
I. Woosnam & P. Broadhurst (2 & 1)	1	0	P. Azinger & H. Irwin
B. Langer & C. Montgomerie (2 & 1)	1	0	C. Pavin & S. Pate
M. James & S. Richardson (3 & 1)	1	0	L. Wadkins & W. Levi
S. Ballesteros & J.-M. Olazábal (halved)	½	½	P. Stewart & F. Couples (halved)
— *SINGLES* —			
N. Faldo (2 holes)	1	0	R. Floyd
D. Feherty (2 & 1)	1	0	P. Stewart
C. Montgomerie (halved)	½	½	M. Calcavecchia (halved)
J.-M. Olazábal	0	1	P. Azinger (2 holes)
S. Richardson	0	1	C. Pavin (2 & 1)
S. Ballesteros (3 & 2)	1	0	W. Levi
I. Woosnam	0	1	C. Beck (3 & 1)
P. Broadhurst (3 & 1)	1	0	M. O'Meara
S. Torrance	0	1	F. Couples (3 & 2)
M. James	0	1	L. Wadkins (3 & 2)
B. Langer (halved)	½	½	H. Irwin (halved)
D. Gilford (DNP)	½	½	S. Pate (injured, DNP)
	13½	**14½**	

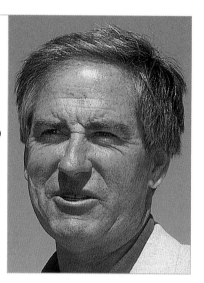

VICTORIOUS CAPTAIN

DAVE STOCKTON

1993

Late September at the Belfry, Sutton Coldfield, could not have been more different from the sweltering heat and windswept shores of Kiawah Island. The cool, grey autumnal skies mirrored the increasingly chilly relationship between the two sides that had grown since the last contest. The bad feeling that had been generated by events at the Ocean Course had been a far cry from Samuel Ryder's founding aims of the Ryder Cup, which he hoped would 'influence a cordial, friendly and peaceful feeling throughout the civilized world'. So it was important that the 30th Ryder Cup made a fresh start and tried to repair some of the damage done two years before.

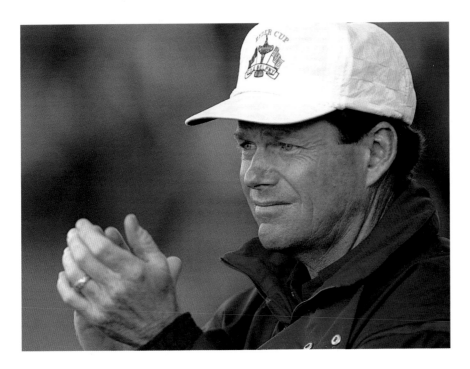

United States captain Tom Watson applauds the efforts of his players.

The choice of Tom Watson as captain of the United States was a good start. His easy charm and steady temperament were seen as the perfect antidote to the gung-ho approach adopted by his predecessor, Dave Stockton. Keen to find out what had gone wrong at Kiawah, Watson sought the advice of, among others, Nick Faldo, who told him that a rise in gamesmanship had peaked at Kiawah Island. He highlighted an incident at the gala dinner where the European team had to sit through an American-edited version of the Ryder Cup history, with every American triumph being greeted with excessive whoops and cheers from its partisan hosts. After some lengthy discussions, Watson concluded that a lowering of the temperature was required, and he set about re-enforcing the philosophy of competitiveness on the course and respect and friendship off it.

Ian Woosnam and Peter Baker celebrate a one-hole win over John Gallacher Jr and Lee Janzen in Friday afternoon's fourballs.

Sadly, these laudable aims were derailed, albeit briefly, by yet another incident at the pre-match gala dinner. During the evening, Sam Torrance, official match programme in hand, wandered over to the American table to ask the players to sign it. It was something of a tradition for the team members to exchange signed programmes before the match, but Watson declined the request. Torrance was incensed, and a diplomatic incident was born. The next day Watson was forced to defend his decision, saying, 'it was taken wrong' and that his team would be happy to sign any programmes that were sent to the US team room. To be fair to Watson, he viewed the dinner as an important bonding session for him and his players and he didn't want to be interrupted by a steady stream of autograph hunters. 'If we sign one, we'd sign for everybody', he reasoned. Torrance though, was still smarting at the refusal: 'it doesn't bear talking about ... I will show you tomorrow what I think. It's just more fuel.' It was a storm in the teacup, but it showed just how fraught relations had become between Europe and the United States. The matches could not start soon enough.

The 1993 competition would be another landmark for the European Tour, with Sweden and Italy becoming the latest countries to produce Ryder Cup players. Joakim Haeggman and Constantino Rocca debuted, along with Barry

Lane and Peter Baker. Woosnam, Faldo, Ballesteros, Olazábal, Montgomerie, James, Langer and Torrance all returned from the 1991 match, and Bernard Gallacher was persuaded to resume his role as captain. The Americans also fielded four rookies: Lee Janzen, John Cook, Davis Love III and Jim Gallagher Jr. Floyd, Couples, Azinger, Pavin, Beck, Stewart, Wadkins and Tom Kite (playing in his seventh and final Ryder Cup) completed the line-up.

After a delayed start due to fog, the first match teed off just after 10.30am. Pavin and Wadkins defeated an off-colour Torrance and James by 4 and 3, then Langer and Woosnam responded with a record win by a European foursome, overwhelming Azinger and Stewart 7 and 5. But the story of the morning was the 2 and 1 defeat of Ballesteros and Olazábal by Kite and Love III. In 13 matches paired together the Spaniards had lost only once before. Ballesteros's golf was a little off colour that morning, and he even resisted the challenge of attempting to drive the short par-four 10th (in the past it had been a signature hole for the Spaniard). Kite seized the opportunity and hit an imperious drive to within 6ft of the hole. Love III duly holed the putt and they didn't look back. Paired together for the first time, Faldo and Montgomerie secured Europe's second point of the morning.

An enthralling afternoon saw Spanish smiles return as Ballesteros and Olazábal exacted a 4 and 3 revenge on Kite and Love III. But it was debutant Peter Baker, playing on his home patch, who delighted the crowds. Partnered by Woosnam, the pair pulled off a thrilling one-hole victory over US rookies Janzen and Gallagher Jr. At the close of play the score was 4–3 in Europe's favour. In the last act of the day, Nick Faldo birdied the 17th to square his and Montgomerie's match with Azinger and Couples. In the fading light the players were called off the course, only to face an anxious night contemplating what would effectively be a one-hole shoot-out down the 18th first thing the next morning.

At 8am the following day the players resumed on the 18th tee. They produced two good drives and two poor ones. It was now Faldo against Azinger. Both made the green with their approaches, but Faldo's long putt finished 10ft short. Sensing a chance, Azinger prowled around the green checking the line, but his putt slid by the hole and he tapped in for par. Faldo scanned the green, settled over his ball and confidently holed the putt. The match was halved.

Nick Faldo punches the air after holing a pressure putt during the fourballs.

By lunch on the second day, Europe had surged into a four-point lead, with only Ray Floyd and partner Payne Stewart managing a win. At 7½–4½, Watson's men were already out of touch, and a bad afternoon would almost certainly prove fatal to their chances. With two points shared in the middle two afternoon fourballs – both Baker and Woosnam and Pavin and Gallagher Jr cruised to massive wins – the Americans really needed both points to stay in the hunt. Faldo, who had started his day by holing from 10ft on the 18th, was required to do exactly the same ten hours later. But the ball didn't drop this time, and Chip Beck and John Cook sneaked a vital point for the United States. Meanwhile, Floyd and Stewart completed their second win of the day, closing out Olazábal and Haeggman on the 17th green to make the score Europe 8½, USA 7½.

On the third morning, Bernard Gallacher would confirm that Sam Torrance, who hadn't played since the first morning, was unfit to play in the singles owing to an infected toe. Two years before, Gallacher had been in the uncomfortable position of telling one of his players (David Gilford) that he would not play in the singles. Now it was Tom Watson's turn to break the bad news to Lanny Wadkins. There had been other dramas too. Peter Baker had spent the night at his daughter's bedside at the local hospital, although thankfully her meningitis scare proved to be just that.

At midday on Sunday, under the gaze of 30,000 spectators, the final matches teed off. Europe made a good start, with Woosnam two up on Couples by the 12th hole and Barry Lane in control at three up with five to play over Chip Beck. But the Americans fought back – Beck especially, who turned his match around in stunning fashion to win by one hole. For his part, Couples converted a two-hole deficit into

Mark James congratulates Payne Stewart who beat him 3 and 2 in the singles. Stewart's was the first of five straight singles victories that saw the United States regain the Ryder Cup.

a half and tied the scores at 9½ points each. Then back came Europe with three wins on the bounce, Montgomerie, Haeggman and Baker all winning at the final hole. Suddenly Europe had 12½ points and needed only two more to regain the Cup. Despite the optimism, the scoreboard was beginning to make grim reading for Europe. The United States was in control in four of the six remaining matches, and it wasn't long before Payne Stewart (3 and 2 winner against Mark James), Tom Kite (5 and 3 winner over Bernhard Langer) and Jim Gallagher Jr (3 and 2 winner over an out-of-form Ballesteros) levelled the scores at 12½ points each. In the final pairing, Nick Faldo was beating Paul Azinger, but it might not matter, as the two matches in front were slipping away from Europe.

Suddenly, all eyes turned to the match between the two rookies. Love III had been edging the match and was one up through the 13th hole. But Rocca responded with back-to-back birdies on the 14th and 15th holes to swing the advantage back to Europe. A tense half at the 16th kept Rocca on course for victory, but the pressure finally told on the Italian at the 17th. Having watched Love III make his par, it looked like a mere formality for Rocca to do the same. But a nervy short putt wriggled past the hole and suddenly the match was all square again. Things for the pair then took on an added significance as news filtered through that Ray Floyd was about to go three up with three to play against José-Maria Olazábal. Europe desperately needed at least a half from Rocca.

It was Love III who now had the momentum though, and he split the 18th fairway with his drive. Rocca's drive found the rough between two fairway bunkers. Staring down a 200yd shot, over water, out of the rough, on debut, in front of a home crowd and to keep your team alive in the Ryder Cup is probably not what Rocca had dreamt of the night before. But he made it over the water, to lie just short of the green. With an easier approach, Love III hit an unspectacular shot but made the putting surface. Rocca hit a nervous chip 25ft past the hole and then two-putted the return, which left Love III, who'd putted up to 6ft, a chance to collect the point and seal overall victory. A perfectly judged right-to-left putt dropped into the middle of the hole. The United States had retained the trophy. The outright win was confirmed when Olazábal hooked his ball into the water at the 18th and 51-year-old Ray Floyd, the oldest man ever to appear in the Ryder Cup, completed a two-hole victory. Paul Azinger ended a miserable day for Europe by snatching a half at the last in his match with Faldo. The final score Europe 13, USA 15.

For the Americans, it was third time lucky at the Belfry. From their lowest point, on Friday lunchtime, they had risen to take ten of the remaining 16 points. Their dominance was such that, on the final afternoon, they quelled the noise from the home crowds, who got the chance to cheer only when the

Peter Baker, who won three out of four points on a sparkling debut at the Belfry.

THE 1990s

RIGHT: *Davis Love III raises his arms triumphantly after holing a 6ft putt that secured overall victory for the United States.*

BELOW: *The victorious United States team: (standing l–r) John Cook, Ray Floyd, Lanny Wadkins, Corey Pavin, Tom Watson (Capt.), Lee Janzen, Payne Stewart, Davis Love III and John Gallagher Jr; (below l–r) Tom Kite, Chip Beck, Paul Azinger and Fred Couples.*

tournament was already slipping away. A joyful and relieved Tom Watson put the achievement in perspective, saying 'This is the finest experience in the game of golf.' It was the highest praise from a great champion.

1993 THE BELFRY GOLF & COUNTRY CLUB, SUTTON COLDFIELD, WEST MIDLANDS

EUROPE			UNITED STATES
FOURSOMES — MORNING			
S. Torrance & M. James	0	1	L. Wadkins & C. Pavin (4 & 3)
I. Woosnam & B. Langer (7 & 5)	1	0	P. Azinger & P. Stewart
S. Ballesteros & J.-M. Olazábal	0	1	T. Kite & D. Love III (2 & 1)
N. Faldo & C. Montgomerie (4 & 3)	1	0	R. Floyd & F. Couples
FOURBALLS — AFTERNOON			
I. Woosnam & P. Baker (1 hole)	1	0	J. Gallagher Jr & L. Janzen
B. Langer & B. Lane	0	1	L. Wadkins & C. Pavin (4 & 2)
N. Faldo & C. Montgomerie (halved)	½	½	P. Azinger & F. Couples (halved)
S. Ballesteros & J.-M. Olazábal (4 & 3)	1	0	D. Love III & T. Kite
FOURSOMES — MORNING			
N. Faldo & C. Montgomerie (3 & 2)	1	0	L. Wadkins & C. Pavin
B. Langer & I. Woosnam (2 & 1)	1	0	F. Couples & P. Azinger
P. Baker & B. Lane	0	1	R. Floyd & P. Stewart (3 & 2)
S. Ballesteros & J.-M. Olazábal (2 & 1)	1	0	D. Love III & T. Kite
FOURBALLS — AFTERNOON			
N. Faldo & C. Montgomerie	0	1	J. Cook & C. Beck (1 hole)
M. James & C. Rocca	0	1	C. Pavin & J. Gallagher Jr (5 & 4)
I. Woosnam & P. Baker (6 & 5)	1	0	F. Couples & P. Azinger
J.-M. Olazábal & J. Haeggman	0	1	R. Floyd & P. Stewart (2 & 1)
SINGLES			
I. Woosnam (halved)	½	½	F. Couples (halved)
B. Lane	0	1	C. Beck (1 hole)
C. Montgomerie (1 hole)	1	0	L. Janzen
P. Baker (2 holes)	1	0	C. Pavin
J. Haeggman (1 hole)	1	0	J. Cook
M. James	0	1	P. Stewart (3 & 2)
C. Rocca	0	1	D. Love III (1 hole)
S. Ballesteros	0	1	J. Gallagher Jr (3 & 2)
J.-M. Olazábal	0	1	R. Floyd (2 holes)
B. Langer	0	1	T. Kite (5 & 3)
N. Faldo (halved)	½	½	P. Azinger (halved)
S. Torrance (injured, DNP)	½	½	L. Wadkins (DNP)

13   15

VICTORIOUS CAPTAIN
TOM WATSON

The two captains, Bernard Gallacher and Lanny Wadkins.

1995

With odds of 2–1 against in a two-horse race, the Europeans were, after two straight defeats, not exactly highly fancied to regain the trophy at Oak Hill in 1995. The parkland course was described by sports journalist Hugh McIlvanney as having been 'calculatingly prepared to provide a butcher's slab on which the Europeans can be dismembered'. Not so the previous year, when Bernard Gallacher, European captain for the third time, had come to inspect it with rival captain Lanny Wadkins. Gallacher described the course then as set up 'as if for a monthly medal', and he asked Wadkins how it might look come the Ryder Cup. 'Pretty much the way you see it', said Wadkins. 'There won't be a lot of difference'. So when Gallacher returned the following May to hear that the greenkeeper had been instructed by the American captain to narrow the fairways, fertilize the rough, grow thick collars of grass around the greens and to have the greens running at 11 on the Stimpmeter, he was more than a little surprised. The course had been prepared to resemble a US Open course, which few Europeans down the years had been granted entry to and even fewer (only Tony Jacklin) had won. In short, the view coming from the Americans was that the Europeans couldn't drive straight, were unfamiliar with delicate lofted chips out of thick rough and had flaky putting skills.

Gallacher's problems didn't end there. Naturally, critics of his captaincy drew comparisons with his predecessor and concluded that the Scot was not authoritarian enough and that he was too reactive. Of course, if he'd won one of the two previous contests the criticism would have been praise. The fact was that the result at Kiawah Island was as close as it could have been, and two years ago at the Belfry Gallacher's most experienced players didn't produce the goods when it mattered on the final day. At the age of 46, Gallacher wasn't about to change his spots, and in any case it was almost certain, win or lose, that this would be his last time in charge.

No sooner had Europe's team been finalized than three players were beginning to look doubtful to start the tournament. Faldo had been suffering from a sore wrist and Ballesteros and Langer both had sore backs. And as only Swedish rookie Per-Ulrik Johansson was under 30 years of age, the team were labelled 'too old' by some critics. Woosnam, Clark, James, Torrance, Montgomerie, Rocca, Gilford and Philip Walton, who debuted, made up the rest of the team.

Wadkins also faced criticism. His wild-card picks, Fred Couples and Curtis Strange, were thought to have been chosen on the basis of friendship with Wadkins, rather than form. Couples, Davis Love III and Corey Pavin were the only three survivors from the 1993 victory. Five rookies – Tom Lehman, Jeff Maggert, Brad Faxon, Lauren Roberts and 25-year-old Phil Mickelson – joined Peter Jacobsen, Ben Crenshaw and Jay Haas in the 31st American team to contest the Ryder Cup.

A rain-sodden opening morning ended with the honours even at 2–2. But after Ballesteros and Gilford had provided a point with a 4 and 3 win over Faxon and Jacobson in the opening afternoon fourball, the Americans proceeded to steamroller their way to a 5–3 lead at the close. Torrance and Rocca, who had gelled so well in the morning, came unstuck against Maggert and Roberts, who thrashed them 6 and 5. Couples and Love III handed Faldo and Montgomerie their second loss of the day, beating the British pair 3 and 2, and Mickelson and Pavin flattened Langer and Johansson 6 and 4. Corey Pavin had done little to endear himself to European golfers with his overindulgent

Corey Pavin celebrates chipping-in at the 18th green, which gave America a 9–7 advantage going into the final-day singles matches.

display of patriotism at Kiawah Island, and at the end of the second day at Oak Hill he would give rise to further annoyance. But this time around he let his clubs do the talking.

Needing a good set of morning foursomes on the second day to reel the Americans back in from their two-point lead, the European's duly delivered three wins out of four to tie the match at six points each. All three victories were comfortable. Faldo and Montgomerie got back in the groove, beating Haas and Strange 4 and 2. Langer and Gilford – who was enjoying a happy return to the Ryder Cup after the misery of 1991 – beat Pavin and Lehman 4 and 3. But the excitement came at the 6th hole when Constantino Rocca, partnered by Torrance, recorded a hole-in-one – only the third in Ryder Cup history – which contributed to a 6 and 5 mauling of Love III and Maggert. Rocca came back well after his tearful dejection at the Belfry.

Rocca also won in the afternoon, this time partnered by Woosnam. But with Couples and Faxon beating Torrance and Montgomerie 4 and 2, and Haas and Mickelson 3 and 2 winners over Ballesteros and Gilford, attention turned to the final match, which would decide the standings going into the singles.

Faldo had begun to run into some form earlier in the day, and partnering Langer fought a nail-biting contest with Pavin and Roberts. Two down after the 8th, Faldo and Langer then halved the deficit at the 9th when the German holed a 10ft putt for par, and on the 10th they drew level. Two holes later the Americans re-established their lead, only to see it wiped out again at the 16th when this time Faldo holed out from 10ft. The match was still all square as the players arrived at the 18th. Faldo's approach settled 15ft away from the hole and the Europeans looked favourites to take it and the match. Roberts had left himself a treacherous 50ft putt and Pavin's ball was on the fringe. Langer, meanwhile, had chipped to 6ft in three. Roberts struck a beautiful putt to 2ft and secured a par, which freed up his partner to go for a birdie. With a wedge, Pavin clipped his ball sweetly off the turf. Moving right to left, the ball caught the left edge of the hole, spun around and dropped for a birdie three. The shot handed the Americans a precious two-point lead going into the singles. Europe had never won from such a position, home or away.

Bernard Gallacher encourages Seve Ballesteros in his match with Tom Lehman, which the American won 4 and 3.

To overturn the odds and the deficit to win back the Ryder Cup, the Europeans would have to put in their best performance in the singles since 1985. Bernard Gallacher took the extraordinary gamble of packing the middle matches with his best players. If the first three starters (Ballesteros, Clark and James) didn't deliver points, the tournament would probably be all over. Clark and James, who hadn't played since the opening morning, came to the party just at the right time. Ballesteros had suffered a disappointing 4 and 3 loss to Lehman, but James struck back immediately with an equivalent win over Maggert and then Clark sweated out a one-hole win over Peter Jacobsen. The two Englishmen had done exactly what had been asked of them, building a platform for the rest of the team.

With Woosnam scraping a half and Rocca losing to his Belfry nemesis Love III 3 and 2, the overall score stood at Europe 9½, USA 11½. In a strange parallel

ABOVE LEFT: *Mark James plays an approach shot during his 4 and 3 win over Jeff Maggert in the singles. James, along with Howard Clark – who beat Peter Jacobsen by one hole – kick- started Europe's march to victory.*

ABOVE: *Nick Faldo watches anxiously as he plays his second shot out of the rough at the 18th hole in his singles match with Curtis Strange.*

with events at the Belfry, the home side was ahead on points but behind in the matches left out on the course. In the space of an hour, Montgomerie, Torrance and Gilford all won for Europe and Pavin beat Langer to tie the match at 12½ points each.

Attention now turned to the match between Faldo and Strange, which had added spice as Strange had beaten Faldo in what had effectively been a shoot-out for the US Open title back in 1988. Having tied for first place, they had embarked upon an 18-hole play-off that Strange had ended up winning comfortably. Not so this Sunday. It was an absorbing battle within a battle, which Strange was edging one up until the 17th. A scrappily played hole – Strange found the right-hand rough and Faldo a greenside bunker – was decided by two par putts. Strange went first, nervously jabbing his ball past the hole. Faldo faced with a similar-length putt, struck it true and the ball dropped into the hole.

All square going down the 450yd par-four 18th, Faldo pulled his drive into the rough on the left-hand side. Strange responded with the perfect drive. Faldo's lie was so bad that he could only hack it forward 100yd. But with the winning line in sight and nerves jangling, Strange played a wretched three-iron short to the right of the green. Still with considerable work to do, Faldo, playing his third shot, had another 100yd to go. Under the pressure of knowing that his match was now the pivotal game in the contest, he played a sublime pitch to 4ft. But it wasn't over yet. Strange played a decent chip up to within 8ft of the hole and had a good chance to make par. He gave his putt every chance to drop, but it stayed out. Faldo had a putt to all but assure victory, and he holed it with trademark authority.

The unlikely figure of Irishman Philip Walton had the honour of sealing the final victory, when he made sure of a one-hole win over Jay Haas with a two-putt on the final green. Earlier that season Walton hadn't been sure he wanted to play in the Ryder Cup because of all the pressure involved. But as Bernard Gallacher rushed on to the 18th green to congratulate him, he realized that his decision to play had been the wisest one of his life.

Lanny Wadkins was inconsolable in defeat and the American press rounded on him for picking two old friends over two in-form younger players – Lee Janzen and Jim Gallagher Jr. Bernard Gallacher had

BELOW LEFT: *Bernard Gallacher leaps for joy as he realizes the Ryder Cup is won.*
BELOW: *Gallacher congratulates Philip Walton after his one-hole win over Jay Haas secures overall victory for Gallacher at his third attempt.*

proved everyone wrong, and had pulled off one of the most remarkable European wins in the history of the competition.

1995 OAK HILL COUNTRY CLUB, ROCHESTER, NEW YORK

VICTORIOUS CAPTAIN

BERNARD GALLACHER

EUROPE			UNITED STATES
— *FOURSOMES* — MORNING			
N. Faldo & C. Montgomerie	0	1	C. Pavin & T. Lehman (1 hole)
S. Torrance & C. Rocca (3 & 2)	1	0	J. Haas & F. Couples
H. Clark & M. James	0	1	D. Love III & J. Maggert (4 & 3)
B. Langer & P.-U. Johansson (1 hole)	1	0	B. Crenshaw & C. Strange
— *FOURBALLS* — AFTERNOON			
D. Gilford & S. Ballesteros (4 & 3)	1	0	B. Faxon & P. Jacobsen
S. Torrance & C. Rocca	0	1	J. Maggert & L. Roberts (6 & 5)
N. Faldo & C. Montgomerie	0	1	F. Couples & D. Love III (3 & 2)
B. Langer & P.-U. Johansson	0	1	C. Pavin & P. Mickelson (6 & 4)
— *FOURSOMES* — MORNING			
N. Faldo & C. Montgomerie (4 & 2)	1	0	C. Strange & J. Haas
S. Torrance & C. Rocca (6 & 5)	1	0	D. Love III & J. Maggert
I. Woosnam & P. Walton	0	1	L. Roberts & P. Jacobsen (1 hole)
B. Langer & D. Gilford (4 & 3)	1	0	C. Pavin & T. Lehman
— *FOURBALLS* — AFTERNOON			
S. Torrance & C. Montgomerie	0	1	B. Faxon & F. Couples (4 & 2)
I. Woosnam & C. Rocca (3 & 2)	1	0	D. Love III & B. Crenshaw
S. Ballesteros & D. Gilford	0	1	J. Haas & P. Mickelson (3 & 2)
N. Faldo & B. Langer	0	1	C. Pavin & L. Roberts (1 hole)
— *SINGLES* —			
S. Ballesteros	0	1	T. Lehman (4 & 3)
H. Clark (1 hole)	1	0	P. Jacobsen
M. James (4 & 3)	1	0	J. Maggert
I. Woosnam (halved)	½	½	F. Couples (halved)
C. Rocca	0	1	D. Love III (3 & 2)
D. Gilford (1 hole)	1	0	B. Faxon
C. Montgomerie (3 & 1)	1	0	B. Crenshaw
N. Faldo (1 hole)	1	0	C. Strange
S. Torrance (2 & 1)	1	0	L. Roberts
B. Langer	0	1	C. Pavin (3 & 2)
P. Walton (1 hole)	1	0	J. Haas
P.-U. Johansson	0	1	P. Mickelson (2 & 1)
	14½	**13½**	

1997

The rain in Spain fell mainly on Valderrama in 1997, as a historic first Ryder Cup on the Continent would be blighted by thunderstorms both before and during the tournament. Seve Ballesteros would cap a brilliant Ryder Cup career by captaining the European team in his homeland. Having left an indelible mark on the competition as a player, the Spaniard was about to impose his considerable character on the job of captaincy, making headlines throughout the week.

Valderrama owner Jaime Ortiz-Patiño greets the players as they arrive in Spain.

The now regular round of pre-match controversy was this year provided by a team selection saga involving Ballesteros's compatriot Miguel Angel Martin. The Spaniard had qualified for the European team by dint of some good results over the previous 18 months, but a wrist injury sustained earlier that season had kept him out of action for several weeks, and he had only returned to the game shortly before the Ryder Cup. With this in mind, Ballesteros asked Martin to take a fitness test, but he refused and within a few hours was informed that he had been deselected. Simple enough it would seem. But Ballesteros actually had an ulterior motive to his request. He had desperately wanted three captain's picks but the rules restricted him to two. With Martin deselected it meant that all his preferred players could now play – Nick Faldo, Jesper Parnevik and his old playing partner José-Maria Olazábal, who had recently returned from a long-standing injury himself.

Martin was understandably upset with the ruling, knowing that he was fit to play. Soon enough, lawyers began circling and legal action was only averted by a very odd compromise. Martin was officially made the 13th 'unofficial' member of the team, posing in photographs, wearing team kit and attending functions. But he didn't play one competitive golf shot all week.

By contrast, the selection of the United States team, captained by Tom Kite, had been a breeze. Many commentators agreed with Kite's assertion that he

The European team: (back row l–r) Miguel-Angel Jimenez (assistant to Seve Ballesteros), Per-Ulrik Johansson, Jesper Parnevik, Colin Montgomerie, Lee Westwood, José-Maria Olazábal, Constantino Rocca, Ian Woosnam and Miguel-Angel Martin; (front row l–r) Bernhard Langer, Thomas Björn, Seve Ballesteros (Capt.), Nick Faldo and Darren Clarke. Ignacio Garrido who played instead of Martin is not pictured.

had a 'dream team'. Although it lacked Cup experience (the players had only 14 appearances between them), it contained six men who had won Major championships – Fred Couples, Lee Janzen, Tom Lehman, Davis Love III and debutants Justin Leonard and Tiger Woods. Along with the stars, the match would mark the debuts of some excellent journeymen professionals – Jim Furyk, Brad Faxon and Scott Hoch. Jeff Maggert, Phil Mickelson and Mark O'Meara, meanwhile, had all served in the team before.

The Europeans fielded their most internationally eclectic team, with a total of six nations: two Spaniards (Ignacio Garrido and Olazábal); two Swedes (Parnevik and Per-Ulrik Johansson); a German (Bernard Langer); a Dane (Thomas Björn); an Italian (Constantino Rocca); and five Britons (Nick Faldo, Ian Woosnam, Colin Montgomerie, Darren Clarke and Lee Westwood).

Ballesteros's influence on proceedings had even extended to the design of the course. Valderrama, located on the Sotogrande Estate in southern Spain, had seen frequent changes to its layout down the years, especially since its colourful owner, Jaime Ortiz-Patiño, had acquired it in 1985. Ballesteros had tweaked the design here and there, but he'd radically altered the layout of the par-five 17th – much to the dismay of the professionals, who loathed it. Colin Montgomerie called it 'the

worst hole we play all year – the worst in Europe', and Mark O'Meara thought some of the changes were an unnecessary gimmick. The source of consternation at the 17th was, in a nutshell, the presence of rough and the lack of it. Ballesteros had completely redesigned the hole, inserting a ribbon of rough that ran across the fairway at precisely the driving distance of most professional golfers (290yd). He had also built a lake that protected the green, and the grass on the banks of the lake was cut so short that a fractional error in line or distance would result in the ball meeting a watery grave.

Heavy overnight rain led to a delayed start, but after ground staff armed with squeegees cleared the course of water, play got underway at 10.30am. The points were shared 2–2 in the morning, but in the afternoon Europe started to

The United States team: (back row l–r) Justin Leonard, Jeff Maggert, Tiger Woods, Brad Faxon, Tom Lehman, Scott Hoch, Fred Couples and Mark O'Meara; (front row l–r) Jim Furyk, Davis Love III, Tom Kite (Capt.), Lee Janzen and Phil Mickelson.

ABOVE: *The groundstaff work frantically to remove surface water from the fairways.*

RIGHT: *Jaime Ortiz-Patiño (centre) oversees preparations to get the course ready after torrential rain.*

pull away from the Americans. Langer and Montgomerie, who'd lost to Woods and O'Meara in the morning fourballs, gained their revenge with an easy 5 and 3 victory in the foursomes. Woods would experience a pretty miserable debut in Spain. He didn't play well all week and managed only 1½ points, when more had been expected of him. The day ended with the scores level at 3–3, and with two matches that would play to a finish the following morning.

The resumption the next day brought Europe a further 1½ points before the start of the scheduled fourballs, Faldo and Westwood completing a 3 and 2 victory over Leonard and Maggert, and Garrido and Parnevik halving with Lehman and Mickelson. A developing feature of the tournament was the sight of captain Ballesteros tearing around in his golf cart 'like a mad scientist', trying to keep up with events in every match.

The second day proper got underway at 10.40am, with the Europeans looking to press home their advantage. But the Americans, perhaps spurred on by the presence of former President George Bush Sr and basketball legend Michael Jordan, took early leads in three of the fourballs and were all square in another. After lunch Europe staged a recovery, chipping away at the leads the United States had established. Montgomerie, partnered by Clarke, levelled the pair's match

Much was expected of Tiger Woods on his Ryder Cup debut, but he only managed 1½ points in 1997.

with Couples and Love III at the 12th and within two hours all the matches were level. Sensing the shift in power, the crowd began to get excited, and when the European putts started dropping to give them leads – Woosnam holed a 30ft putt to go two up and Montgomerie holed from 20ft to go one up – Valderrama was abuzz. More was to come: Faldo and Westwood handed Woods and O'Meara their second successive defeat at the 17th (Woods putted into the water); and when Olazábal holed from 20ft to snatch him and Garrido a half with Mickelson and Lehman, the peripatetic Ballesteros, who had stopped long enough to watch the conclusion, jumped around in delight. Europe now had a four-point lead.

RIGHT: *Seve Ballesteros could not keep still during the matches at Valderrama. Here he enjoys a more pensive moment.*

BELOW: *No margin for error at the controversial 17th hole. Tiger Woods putted into the water on the second day.*

As the schedule had been severely disrupted owing to the weather, only one of the foursomes played to a finish on Saturday. At dusk, Montgomerie and Langer sealed yet another point against Furyk and Janzen to leave the overnight score standing at Europe 9, USA 4.

On the final morning honours were shared in the remaining three foursomes, leaving Europe needing just four points for outright victory. In the end that was all they managed, but their victory was never in much doubt. Kite sent out his best players first, and although Couples trounced Woosnam 8 and 7, the American team couldn't close the points gap sufficiently. In the second match Swede Per-Ulrik Johansson beat Love III, soon followed by Constantino Rocca's win over a despondent Tiger Woods 4 and 2. The United States fought back with three consecutive victories, but with Langer securing a point on the 17th green, beating Brad Faxon 2 and 1, the Cup had been regained by the Europeans. Jim Furyk and Tom Lehman gave the US the chance of drawing the

A keen supporter of golf and, in particular, the Ryder Cup, the Duke of York listens as Seve Ballesteros imparts some golfing wisdom.

match, but Montgomerie, needing a half at the 18th to secure the win, was steady as a rock. He collected his par four with ease, while Scott Hoch made a hash of it. Montgomerie, knowing he'd secured victory for Europe, generously gave Hoch his 12ft putt for par to halve the hole.

RIGHT: *Seve Ballesteros congratulates Colin Montgomerie after he and Darren Clarke secure a one-hole victory over Fred Couples and Davis Love III in the second-day foursomes.*

BELOW: *The match finished as it had begun. The European players with the trophy and rain pouring down from leaden skies – not that it dampened the celebrations.*

Ballesteros had realized his dream. 'This is very special', he said. 'Having the Ryder Cup in Spain and being captain, and then winning – I don't think I can have anymore.' It was a fitting finale to what would be the end of his Ryder Cup career.

1997 VALDERRAMA GOLF CLUB, SOTOGRANDE, SPAIN

EUROPE			UNITED STATES
— *FOURSOMES* — MORNING			
J.-M. Olazábal & C. Rocca (1 up)	1	0	D. Love III & P. Mickelson
N. Faldo & L. Westwood	0	1	F. Couples & B. Faxon (1 up)
J. Parnevik & P.-U. Johansson (1 up)	1	0	T. Lehman & J. Furyk
C. Montgomerie & B. Langer	0	1	T. Woods & M. O'Meara (3 & 2)
— *FOURBALLS* — AFTERNOON			
C. Rocca & J.-M. Olazábal	0	1	S. Hoch & L. Janzen (1 up)
B. Langer & C. Montgomerie (5 & 3)	1	0	M. O'Meara & T. Woods
N. Faldo & L. Westwood (3 & 2)	1	0	J. Leonard & J. Maggert
J. Parnevik & I. Garrido (halved)	½	½	T. Lehman & P. Mickelson (halved)
— *FOURSOMES* — MORNING			
C. Montgomerie & D. Clarke (1 up)	1	0	F. Couples & D. Love III
I. Woosnam & T. Björn (2 & 1)	1	0	J. Leonard & B. Faxon
N. Faldo & L. Westwood (2 & 1)	1	0	T. Woods & M. O'Meara
J.-M. Olazábal & I. Garrido (halved)	½	½	P. Mickelson & T. Lehman (halved)
— *FOURBALLS* — AFTERNOON			
C. Montgomerie & B. Langer (1 up)	1	0	L. Janzen & J. Furyk
N. Faldo & L. Westwood	0	1	S. Hoch & J. Maggert (2 & 1)
J. Parnevik & I. Garrido (halved)	½	½	J. Leonard & T. Woods (halved)
J.-M. Olazábal & C. Rocca (5 & 4)	1	0	D. Love III & F. Couples
— *SINGLES* —			
I. Woosnam	0	1	F. Couples (8 & 7)
P.-U. Johansson (3 & 2)	1	0	D. Love III
J. Parnevik	0	1	M. O'Meara (5 & 4)
D. Clarke	0	1	P. Mickelson (2 & 1)
C. Rocca (4 & 2)	1	0	T. Woods
T. Björn (halved)	½	½	J. Leonard (halved)
I. Garrido	0	1	T. Lehman (7 & 6)
B. Langer (2 & 1)	1	0	B. Faxon
L. Westwood	0	1	J. Maggert (3 & 2)
J.-M. Olazábal	0	1	L. Janzen (1 up)
N. Faldo	0	1	J. Furyk (3 & 2)
C. Montgomerie (halved)	½	½	S. Hoch (halved)
14½		**13½**	

VICTORIOUS CAPTAIN
SEVE BALLESTEROS

TOP: *The two captains Ben Crenshaw and Mark James share a joke at the start of the 33rd Ryder Cup at The Country Club, Brookline.*

ABOVE: *Ben Crenshaw wears the Ryder Cup ring, which is given to all American players after a victory. In 1999 Crenshaw presented the players with rings before the match began.*

1999

The last Ryder Cup of the 20th century went off with an almighty bang, and yet it had all started so cordially. No sooner had Europe's captain, Mark James, stepped off Concorde at Boston's Logan Airport than he was issuing declarations of civility: 'We have come to one of the most beautiful cities in America … and we are playing one of the best golf courses. Although we are hoping to retain the trophy, the main thing is that we all have a good week.' US captain Ben Crenshaw added, 'The captain does not have to impart much about sportsmanship. Golfers generally comport themselves very well.' All week leading up to the match, these sentiments were reiterated by both captains, in the hope that the over-the-top celebrations and gamesmanship that had tarnished the match at Kiawah Island would not be repeated at the Country Club in Brookline. But the European and American teams were never going to walk off into the sunset together or even to the nearest bar to share a beer, and what would turn out to be a dramatic contest ended in controversy.

Before leaving Britain, Mark James had surprised everyone by not selecting Nick Faldo to play. His two wild-card picks were the relatively inexperienced Jesper Parnevik (34 years old and with one cap) and Andrew Coltart (a 29-year-old rookie). Faldo's absence would end a sequence of 11 straight appearances stretching back 22 years to 1977. There was no room either for two other Cup veterans, Bernhard Langer and Ian Woosnam, who had 17 appearances between them and were overlooked in favour of players that made up what would be the most inexperienced European team ever to have flown to the United States. Over half the team members were rookies: Frenchman Jean Van De Velde, fresh from his troubles at the Open at Carnoustie; Paul Lawrie, the Open Champion; the Finn Jarmo Sandelin; Irishman Padraig Harrington; and two Spaniards, Miguel Angel

Jimenez and 19-year-old Sergio Garcia. José-Maria Olazábal was now the most experienced player, with five tournaments to his name, followed by Colin Montgomerie with four. Lee Westwood and Darren Clarke, who had debuted at Valderrama, also both returned for duty.

The media were on the lookout for any cracks in the cordial veneer, and they soon found a story. After finishing a practice round, experienced Cup player Jeff Maggert idly boasted in an interview that the United States had an unbeatable team. In an echo of Ben Hogan's famous words in 1967, and Ray Floyd's infamous rehash at the Belfry in 1989, Maggert told reporters, 'Let's face it, we've got the 12 best players in the world.' The media immediately seized on the comment and pressed the European captain for a response. 'I've always said the world rankings are wrong. I'm glad Jeff agrees with me', James said, a comment that immediately took the heat out of a potential flash point. Maggert's bravado wasn't helped by his world ranking of 18.

Nonetheless, the United States was fielding its strongest team in many years. Only David Duval was making his debut, the rest of the players having accumulated 25 appearances between them. The team of Lehman, Sutton, Mickelson, Love III, Woods, O'Meara, Pate, Leonard, Stewart, Furyk and Maggert were firm favourites to regain the trophy.

Despite their favourites tag and supportive home crowd, the Americans could only watch as Europe confounded all the predictions and surged ahead in the opening-day foursome/fourball matches to lead 6–2 by the end of play. It was the worst American start since Muirfield Village in 1987, and they didn't need reminding of how that finished. None of their much talked-up 'big guns' (Woods, Duval, Mickelson, Love III and Leonard) won a match all day. The biggest disappointment for Crenshaw was the pairing of Woods and Duval, who were the top two ranked players in the world. Their partnership had misfired and over the closing holes it was their opponents, Clarke and Westwood, who held their nerve best. With two holes to play, the match was all square. In the fading light Clarke had played an exquisite chip to the 17th green to grab the lead, and on the last hole Westwood chipped close to ensure par and victory.

Earlier on in the day, Europe had taken a 2½–1½ lead into lunch. Montgomerie and Lawrie claimed the team's first point by beating Duval and Mickelson 3 and 2, but it was the pairing of Parnevik and Garcia that caught the

Jesper Parnevik and Sergio Garcia were unbeatable in the fourballs and foursomes matches at Brookline. Here they celebrate a chip-in by Parnevik.

The Bush Family: (l–r) George W, Jeb, George Bush Sr and Barbara. George W Bush (then Governor of Texas) gave his rousing 'Battle of the Alamo' speech to the United States team on the eve of the singles matches.

eye. Having beaten Lehman and Woods in the morning 2 and 1, they faced Mickelson and Furyk in the afternoon. Parnevik, particularly, was in breathtaking form. In the first ten holes the Swede had made five birdies and a glorious eagle, which came courtesy of a 100yd wedge shot that landed in the hole. The Americans fought back and took the match to the final hole, but they couldn't halt what was turning into a European march. Olazábal and Jimenez beat Sutton and Maggert 2 and 1 to make the score 5–2, and Clarke and Westwood did the rest. Afterwards, Crenshaw was philosophical: 'this is what happens in matchplay, there is ebb and flow, ebb and flow'. James wasn't getting carried away either: 'It's just one day out of three', he told reporters.

The Europeans maintained their four-point lead throughout the second day. For a short while they even had a five-point lead as the second pairing of Clarke and Westwood continued their unbeatable form to dispatch Furyk and O'Meara 3 and 2. Up ahead, however, Sutton and Maggert closed out Montgomerie and Lawrie on the 18th green to win one up. In Steve Pate, Woods found a partner he could do business with. They struggled against Harrington and Jimenez until the 14th, where they took the lead and hung on until the last hole.

The afternoon belonged once again to Parnevik and Garcia, whose hard-won half point must have felt more like a full point. Their opponents, Duval and

An anxious Ben Crenshaw has much to think about as Europe surge into a 10–6 lead going into the final day singles.

Love III, were up in the match on four occasions but could not close out the Europeans. And when Garcia holed a 10ft putt at the 18th to claim the half, it was Europe who celebrated, leaving Duval and Love III to ponder the chances they had squandered. For Europe, the only disappointing aspect of the day was the increasing amount of heckling from the American spectators. Montgomerie,

Colin Montgomerie was the subject of persistent abuse from some members of the American crowd at Brookline. He dealt with it admirably, losing only one match out of five.

in particular, was singled out for the coarsest of abuse, which even led some of the more polite sections of the American crowd to condemn the hecklers openly.

With the score at 10–6 in Europe's favour at the end of the second day, the Americans had a mountain to climb. Crenshaw had moved from a philosophical viewpoint to a spiritual one: 'I'm a big believer in fate', he announced at the press conference, continuing 'I have a good feeling about this.' Later that evening, he famously enlisted the more earthly help of the then Governor of Texas, George W. Bush Jr, who travelled to the players' hotel to make a rousing speech – Bush later joked that he was going to remind them to keep their left arm straight. He read from William Travis's letter from the Battle of the Alamo: 'I have sustained a continual bombardment and cannonade for 24 hours & have not lost a man. The enemy has demanded a surrender at discretion … I have answered the demand with a cannon shot and our flag still waves proudly from the walls. I shall never surrender or retreat …Victory or death.'

For Crenshaw, the Fates proved kind to him. His team achieved the greatest comeback in Ryder Cup history, winning 8½ out of 12 points on offer. It was a staggering revival. Collectively, the Americans were 38 under par for the day, compared to Europe's ten. The Americans ambushed Europe in the top six singles matches, Lehman, Sutton, Mickelson, Love III, Woods and Duval all feeding off the crowds. And as putts dropped and chips popped into the hole, the roars echoed around the Country Club. Two days of defeats for David Duval had turned into fist-pumping victory and Tiger Woods had come alive at last. No match went past the 16th, and in the space of an hour the United States had 12 points to Europe's 10.

Harrington collected Europe's first point of the day in the seventh match when he beat Mark O'Meara at the last hole. But almost immediately, Steve Pate restored the two-point margin, beating Jimenez 2 and 1. With Furyk closing in on victory in the 11th match, it was now guaranteed that the Americans could not lose the tournament, but they needed at least a half from one other match to regain the trophy. Up stepped Jason Leonard.

Leonard's stunning revival was a microcosm of the Americans' day. With eight holes left to play in his match against Olazábal, the 24-year-old Texan was four down and seemingly out of it. But then he started holing putts and, having halved the deficit with wins on the 11th and 12th, he proceeded to make birdies at the 13th and 14th holes to square the match. To the understandable delight of the crowd, the American was now looking favourite to win. Olazábal then managed to stem the tide by halving the next two holes, and so the match arrived at the 17th green all square.

Olazábal had played the better shot into the green, leaving himself a 20ft birdie chance. Leonard, meanwhile, suddenly feeling some nerves, had left his ball 45ft away towards the front of the green. This was now the 'swing match' in the Ryder Cup, and both the European and the American team members were crouched down at the back of the green watching events. Leonard struck his putt. The ball came racing

THE 1990s

BELOW: *Countdown to controversy.*
All square in his match against
José-Maria Olazábal, Justin Leonard
sends his amazing putt on its way at the
17th green.

up the slope and on to the flat and then dropped. He raised his arms in the air
and started running around celebrating. In the excitement of the moment, all
the American players charged across the green like stampeding cattle. They
were jumping around, punching the air and screaming in celebration. Even
their wives started joining in, and for several minutes the 17th green was
pandemonium. Meanwhile, Olazábal was leaning on his putter, waiting to putt.
The match wasn't over and he could still halve the hole. The celebrations had
been premature.

  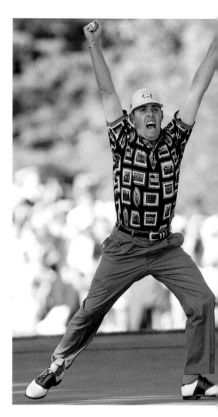

OPPOSITE PAGE

TOP: *United States players storm onto*
the 17th green after Justin Leonard
holes his monster putt. Olazábal
(centre) still had a putt to halve the hole.

BOTTOM: *The victorious United States*
team.

When all the Americans had left the green, Olazábal was finally allowed to
putt. He missed. And with Leonard now dormie one, the celebrations could
officially begin. Montgomerie was subjected to further abuse from the spectators,
but nonetheless he managed to beat Payne Stewart by 1 hole. Paul Lawrie also
beat Jeff Maggert in the final game, easily winning 4 and 3, but it was all too late
for the Europeans. The Americans had played out of their skins and the
European team rightfully acknowledged this fact. However, the events on the
17th green left a bad taste in the mouth, and Tom Lehman was even accused of
running over the line of Olazábal's putt. For all the angry words spoken
afterwards, it was José-Maria Olazábal who summoned the right ones for the
situation: 'It was very sad to see. Showing emotions is fine, but we are trying to
show respect to one another. It would be for the benefit of golf if we all manage

to behave a little better at the Belfry.' Unbeknown to everyone, the Belfry would be three years away, as world events would put the squabbles over a game of golf into perspective.

1999 THE COUNTRY CLUB, BROOKLINE, BOSTON, MASSACHUSETTS

EUROPE			UNITED STATES
— FOURSOMES — MORNING			
P. Lawrie & C. Montgomerie (3 & 2)	1	0	D. Duval & P. Mickelson
S. Garcia & J. Parnevik (2 & 1)	1	0	T. Lehman & T. Woods
M.A. Jimenez & P. Harrington (halved)	½	½	D. Love III & P. Stewart (halved)
D. Clarke & L. Westwood	0	1	J. Maggert & H. Sutton (3 & 2)
— FOURBALLS — AFTERNOON			
S. Garcia & J. Parnevik (1 hole)	1	0	J. Furyk & P. Mickelson
C. Montgomerie & P. Lawrie (halved)	½	½	J. Leonard & D. Love III (halved)
M.A. Jimenez & J.M. Olazábal (2 & 1)	1	0	J. Maggert & H. Sutton
D. Clarke & L. Westwood (1 hole)	1	0	D. Duval & T. Woods
— FOURSOMES — MORNING			
P. Lawrie & C. Montgomerie	0	1	J. Maggert & H. Sutton (1 hole)
D. Clarke & L. Westwood (3 & 2)	1	0	J. Furyk & M. O'Meara
M.A. Jimenez & P. Harrington	0	1	S. Pate & T. Woods (1 hole)
S. Garcia & J. Parnevik (3 & 2)	1	0	J. Leonard & P. Stewart
— FOURBALLS — AFTERNOON			
D. Clarke & L. Westwood	0	1	P. Mickelson & T. Lehman (2 & 1)
S. Garcia & J. Parnevik (halved)	½	½	D. Love III & D. Duval (halved)
M.A. Jimenez & J.M. Olazábal (halved)	½	½	J. Leonard & H. Sutton (halved)
P. Lawrie & C. Montgomerie (2 & 1)	1	0	S. Pate & T. Woods
— SINGLES —			
L. Westwood	0	1	T. Lehman (3 & 2)
D. Clarke	0	1	H. Sutton (4 & 2)
J. Sandelin	0	1	P. Mickelson (4 & 3)
J. Van De Velde	0	1	D. Love III (6 & 5)
A. Coltart	0	1	T. Woods (3 & 2)
J. Parnevik	0	1	D. Duval (5 & 4)
P. Harrington (1 hole)	1	0	M. O'Meara
M.A. Jimenez	0	1	S. Pate (2 & 1)
J.M. Olazábal (halved)	½	½	J. Leonard (halved)
C. Montgomerie (1 hole)	1	0	P. Stewart
S. Garcia	0	1	J. Furyk (4 & 3)
P. Lawrie (4 & 3)	1	0	J. Maggert
	13½	**14½**	

VICTORIOUS CAPTAIN
BEN CRENSHAW

FROM ODD TO EVEN

2002–2004

2002

The terrorist attacks on New York's Twin Towers on 11 September 2001 left in their wake a prolonged sense of shock and bewilderment. The Ryder Cup was scheduled to start at the Belfry just 17 days after the tragedy, and so it was inevitable that the staging of the tournament would be thrown into doubt. In light of the obvious fears over safety, there were two conflicting opinions as to what course of action would be deemed appropriate. On the one hand, cancelling the Ryder Cup and stopping the business of getting on with life would, some argued, hand the terrorists a victory. On the other, there was the opinion that, out of respect for the dead and the family and friends they left behind, the match should at least be postponed. Alternatively, as previous European captain Mark James suggested, the event could be cancelled and the teams could wait until the next match in 2003.

The two capains, Sam Torrance and Curtis Strange.

Officials at the respective PGAs in Britain and America remained tight-lipped over the matter for six days, causing the media to bay at their doors and instigating a period of wild speculation about what might, should or would happen. Players who were due to take part in the match were canvassed for their opinions. Most of them agreed that a postponement of at least a few months was the right path to take. On Monday, 17 September 2001, the PGAs announced that the match would be postponed for exactly one year and that from now on the Ryder Cup would be played every even calendar year. Both team captains – Sam Torrance and Curtis Strange – agreed to play the same 12 men that had originally been picked for the 2001 competition.

With the bumped-up security and all the signage around the Belfry still showing the date 2001, the 34th Ryder Cup was a depressing reminder of the

Opening ceremony 2002. Prayers are said for the victims of the terrorist attacks on 11 September 2001.

consequences of terrorism. The perimeter cordon was manned by 45 armed police officers and rigorous airport-style checks were enforced for every one of the 35,000 spectators in a security operation that was unprecedented for a sporting event.

OPPOSITE PAGE

TOP LEFT: *Montgomerie practises at the Belfry. All signage remained as it would have been for the 2001 competition.*

TOP RIGHT: *Sergio Garcia and Sam Torrance share a joke. Garcia's pairing with Lee Westwood yielded three points out of a possible four.*

BOTTOM: *Spectators flock to the 10th green – one of the greatest matchplay holes in golf.*

Before the tournament started, the two captains were keen to adopt the right tone. 'I think leading up to the matches we're going to remember why we're a year late', said Curtis Strange. 'We should never forget why we're playing this year. But I've always said once the tee goes in the ground Friday morning, I think you're going to see a good, solid match.' Sam Torrance echoed the words of his opposite number, saying 'This is going to be very competitive, trust me. The Ryder Cup is the Ryder Cup.' A solemn opening ceremony remembered the victims of 11 September and also Payne Stewart, who had died in an air accident a month after the match at Brookline.

As the usual pre-match jousting between the two sides was distinctly muted, it fell to Tiger Woods to supply the controversy with comments he made two weeks before the competition got underway. Playing in the American Express Championship at Mount Juliet in Ireland, he suggested that he would rather win its $1 million dollar first prize than the Ryder Cup. It was not his favourite golf event, he added, complaining that his own routines were disrupted by

Colin Montgomerie takes the applause at the 14th green as he completes a crushing 5 and 4 victory over Scott Hoch in the first singles match.

OPPOSITE PAGE

TOP: *Philip Price (World ranked 119) holes the putt on the 16th green that secures a 3 and 2 victory over World No.2 Phil Mickelson.*

BOTTOM: *Paul Azinger celebrates with his caddie after holing out from the bunker at the 18th, to secure a half point against Nicholas Fasth and postpone Europe's victory*

having to attend all the various functions. Perhaps the usually media-savvy Woods should have known better than to air such feelings, because his words were seized on and spun to portray him as unpatriotic and detached from his team-mates.

Any hope Woods might have had of creating some more positive headlines were dashed when he failed to register a single point on the first day. Sent out with Paul Azinger in the morning fourballs, Woods and his partner played well enough to record a combined total of nine under par for the round. However, their opponents, Darren Clarke and Thomas Björn, were one better on ten under and ended up one-hole winners. Woods tried his luck with Mark Calcavecchia in the afternoon, but if anything he fared worse, twice missing 3ft putts to hand the initiative to Lee Westwood and Sergio Garcia, who ran out 2 and 1 winners.

It wasn't just Woods who was having a hard time of it that morning. His team-mates could manage only one point courtesy of a one-hole win for Mickelson and Toms over Padraig Harrington and Nicholas Fasth. But after Curtis Strange rejigged the pairings at lunchtime, the Americans' fortunes improved in the afternoon, when they gained 2½ points to Europe's 1½. By the end of the day they had closed the gap to finish just 4½–3½ down.

The second day came alive in the afternoon fourballs after the teams shared the points in the morning. Mickelson and Toms maintained their 100 per cent record, beating Fulke and Price, and after a dismal first day Tiger Woods found harmony in his partnership with Davis Love III, the pair overwhelming Clarke and Björn 4 and 3. Montgomerie and Langer won again, as did Garcia and Westwood. The Englishman was enjoying a welcome return to form after having slumped from being the world no. 5 at Brookline in 1999 to no. 148 at the Belfry three years later.

It was difficult to know how the points would be shared out in the afternoon, such was the seesaw nature of all four matches. An out-of-form Jesper Parnevik partnered Nicholas Fasth against Calcavecchia and Duval. The Europeans charged into a three-hole lead after eight holes, but when Duval became the first player of the week to drive the green from the back tee at the

10th, the United States hit the comeback trail and ground out a one-hole win.

Montgomerie, partnered by Harrington, repeated the imperious form he had shown all week, beating the previously unconquered pairing of Mickelson and Toms. 'I've never played better than that,' said the Scot after the 2 and 1 victory, 'and it had to be so because we were playing the second- and sixth-ranked players in the world.'

Westwood and Garcia, victorious over Woods and Calcavecchia on the Friday, were once again in inspired form and looked on course to beat the world no. 1 in a memorable match. Confirming his return to form, Westwood collected six birdies during his round, including one at the 10th where he and Garcia both drove the green, much to the delight of the crowd. The match turned dramatically on the 17th. Davis Love III levelled by chipping in for a birdie as Garcia three-putted. The Americans then pocketed an unlikely but priceless point when Westwood missed from 4ft on the last. 'We all played well today, it was a great match', said Woods, who was eight under on his own.

FROM ODD TO EVEN

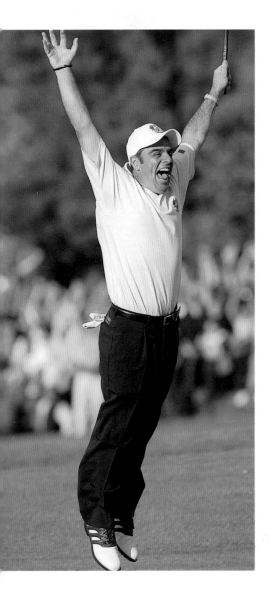

Paul McGinley leaps for joy
after holing the putt that gave
Europe victory.

In the last match on the second day, Paul McGinley and Darren Clarke fought back from two down with four holes to play, winning the next two holes to square against Hoch and Furyk. Hoch then birdied the 17th to make the Americans look odds-on for the point and, crucially, a lead going into the last day. But McGinley holed a vital par putt at the last to snatch a half point, sending the galleries home with something to cheer about. Little did McGinley know that he'd be back in 24 hours time to hole an equally vital putt.

At the end of day two the competition was tied at 8–8. As the United States was historically superior in the singles, this meant that the Europeans might be one or two points shy of the total they needed at the start of the day. But Torrance had a plan. He surprised everyone when he read out his singles order, as he had packed the top half with his best players. Montgomerie would lead off, followed by Garcia, Clarke, Langer, Harrington and Björn. Strange, on the other hand, had put all his strength at the bottom, with the top two players in the world, Woods and Mickelson, last. It seemed that Strange had been outwitted. Following the example of Crenshaw at Brookline, Torrance had gambled everything on the first six matches.

At 11.15am, Colin Montgomerie stood on the 1st tee and was greeted by deafening cheers as his name was read out by the starter. It was to set the tone for the rest of the day. He immediately went one up on his opponent, Scott Hoch, who was never really in the match. Two and half hours later Europe had its first point, Montgomerie bashfully acknowledging the cheers that greeted his win on the 14th green. The Scot had won 4½ points out of 5, playing the Ryder Cup of his life. In 82 holes of golf, not once had he been behind.

Although Sergio Garcia lost his match to David Toms at the last hole, Torrance's strategy had worked. Langer, Harrington and Björn all delivered wins against Sutton, Calcavecchia and Cink. Clarke then halved his match with Duval to give Europe 12½ points. With Westwood losing to Verplank, Europe needed to find two points from the remaining five matches. An unlikely hero emerged to provide the upset of the day.

Welshman Philip Price, ranked 119th in the world, was playing against Phil Mickelson, ranked at no. 2. Everyone thought it would be a gimme for Mickelson and Price was given no chance. But he outplayed the American, sinking five birdie putts, the fifth and final one on the 16th green. With a putt to win the match, Price rattled the ball in and put Europe on the brink of victory. 'I didn't think I had it in me,' he said afterwards, 'but I'm glad to find I have.'

Up ahead on the 18th, Nicholas Fasth was one-up against Paul Azinger, and looked certain to secure the point that would regain the Ryder Cup for Europe. That was until Azinger holed out from the greenside bunker to claim a birdie and a vital half point for America, leaving Europe on the brink of outright victory.

Azinger' heroics had provided Paul McGinley with the unexpected opportunity to secure a place in history. Coming down the 18th, the Irishman

was all-square with Jim Furyk. Both players had pulled their approaches left of the green. McGinley found the rough, Furyk, the bunker. McGinley played a delicate chip, leaving himself a 10ft putt for par. Furyk almost gave the on-looking Sam Torrance a heart attack as he came within in a whisker of repeating Azinger's sensational bunker shot moments earlier.

McGinley now had a putt for the Ryder Cup. Calmly, he eased the ball into the hole. Jumping with delight, he was joined by Torrance and the rest of the team on the green. With Tiger Woods still out on the course, his match with Parnevik an irrelevance, the Europeans began to celebrate. Two halves in the last two matches had given them victory by two points, and Torrance's gamble had paid off handsomely. 'What a team. What a team', said the emotional captain. 'All I did was lead them to the water … they drank copiously.'

Everyone was in agreement about who had been the star of the week. Even Curtis Strange, who was not only gracious but generous and sincere in defeat,

ABOVE LEFT: *Padraig Harrington tries to pick up Paul McGinley as the two Irishmen celebrate Europe's 15½–12½ win at the Belfry.*

INSET: *Sergio Garcia rushes onto the 18th green as Paul McGinley holes the winning putt.*

ABOVE LEFT: *Victory is sweet. Sam Torrance caps a wonderful Ryder Cup career as winning captain.*

said, 'Seve was their leader for a long time. Now it's Colin.' Eleven years after making his debut at Kiawah Island, Montgomerie was, as Torrance put it, 'king of the castle'.

2002 — THE BELFRY GOLF & COUNTRY CLUB, SUTTON COLDFIELD, WEST MIDLANDS

EUROPE			UNITED STATES
— FOURBALLS — MORNING			
D. Clarke & T. Björn (1 hole)	1	0	T. Woods & P. Azinger
S. Garcia & L. Westwood (4 & 3)	1	0	D. Duval & D. Love III
C. Montgomerie & B. Langer (4 & 3)	1	0	S. Hoch & J. Furyk
P. Harrington & N. Fasth	0	1	P. Mickelson & D. Toms (1 hole)
— FOURSOMES — AFTERNOON			
D. Clarke & T. Björn	0	1	H. Sutton & S. Verplank (2 & 1)
S. Garcia & L. Westwood (2 & 1)	1	0	T. Woods & M. Calcavecchia
C. Montgomerie & B. Langer (halved)	½	½	P. Mickelson & D. Toms (halved)
P. Harrington & P. McGinley	0	1	S. Cink & J. Furyk (3 & 2)
— FOURSOMES — MORNING			
P. Fulke & P. Price	0	1	P. Mickelson & D. Toms (2 & 1)
S. Garcia & L. Westwood (2 & 1)	1	0	J. Furyk & S. Cink
C. Montgomerie & B. Langer (1 hole)	1	0	S. Verplank & S. Hoch
D. Clarke & T. Björn	0	1	T. Woods & D. Love III (4 & 3)
— FOURBALLS — AFTERNOON			
N. Fasth & J. Parnevik	0	1	M. Calcavecchia & D. Duval (1 hole)
C. Montgomerie & P. Harrington (2 & 1)	1	0	P. Mickelson & D. Toms
S. Garcia & L. Westwood	0	1	T. Woods & D. Love III (1 hole)
D. Clarke & P. McGinley (halved)	½	½	S. Hoch & J. Furyk (halved)
— SINGLES —			
C. Montgomerie (5 & 4)	1	0	S. Hoch
S. Garcia	0	1	D. Toms (1 hole)
D. Clarke (halved)	½	½	D. Duval (halved)
B. Langer (4 & 3)	1	0	H. Sutton
P. Harrington (5 & 4)	1	0	M. Calcavecchia
T. Björn (2 & 1)	1	0	S. Cink
L. Westwood	0	1	S. Verplank (2 & 1)
N. Fasth (halved)	½	½	P. Azinger (halved)
P. McGinley (halved)	½	½	J. Furyk (halved)
P. Fulke (halved)	½	½	D. Love III (halved)
P. Price (3 & 2)	1	0	P. Mickelson
J. Parnevik (halved)	½	½	T. Woods (halved)

15½	**12½**

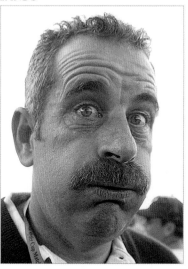

VICTORIOUS CAPTAIN

SAM TORRANCE

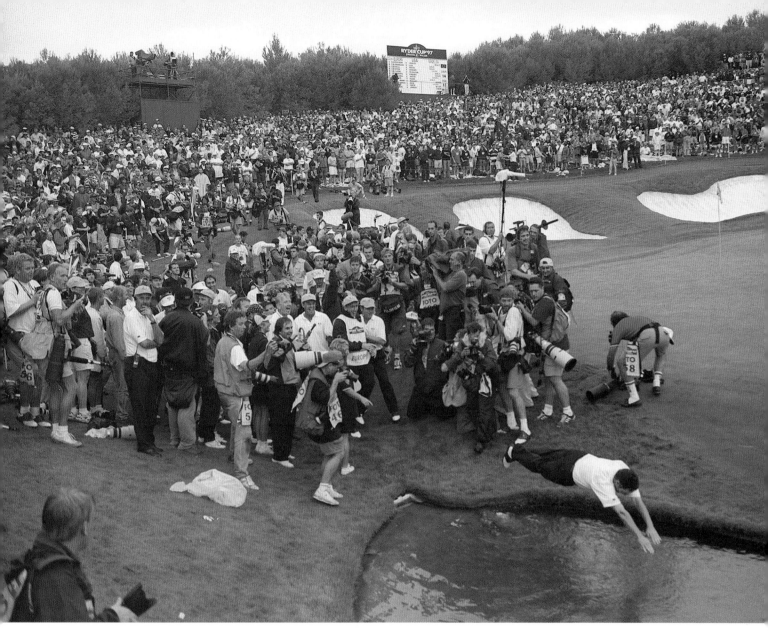

FROM ODD TO EVEN

The two captains, Bernhard Langer and Hal Sutton.

OPPOSITE PAGE

TOP: *Tiger Woods and Phil Mickelson on the first morning in their match with Colin Montgomerie and Padraig Harrington. What Hal Sutton had called his 'dream team' had a nightmare.*

BOTTOM: *The 'walking soundbite' Hal Sutton ponders a question at one of his entertaining press conferences.*

2004

Sixty-four years after playing host to the first unofficial Ryder Cup match of World War II, Oakland Hills near Detroit became the 28th course to host an official Ryder Cup match. When Walter Hagen's Ryder Cuppers and Gene Sarazen's Challengers lined up against each other in 1940, it was to raise money for the American Red Cross. Hagen's team – the 1939 American Ryder Cup team – won that match 7–5. For the American class of 2004, Oakland Hills wouldn't prove such a happy hunting ground.

Although the Americans started the match as favourites (as they always did on home soil), there wasn't much to choose between the two teams. The United States did have five Major winners in the side, but past Ryder Cups had often rendered this statistic obsolete – one needed only to look at the Ryder Cup record of Tiger Woods to spring a leak in that theory. And as Europe had often proved in the past, a good team ethic was just as important as individual talent.

If there wasn't much to choose between the two teams, the captains more than made up for it. Bernhard Langer and Hal Sutton were two men so different that it's difficult to know where to start. The wiry-framed Langer was a meticulous planner and a thinker, while steak-framed Sutton was a big-picture man and walking sound bite.

Both teams had five rookies coming into the match: Paul Casey, Luke Donald, Ian Poulter, Thomas Levet and David Howell for Europe; and Kenny Perry, Chad Campbell, Chris DiMarco, Fred Funk and Chris Riley for the United States. Langer had chosen Colin Montgomerie and Luke Donald for his wild cards. Montgomerie had been having a miserable time of it both on and off the course that year, with the break-up of his marriage signalling a slump in his form, but his presence at a Ryder Cup was now mandatory, such was his record. Rookie Luke Donald, meanwhile, was one of the cleanest ball-strikers in the game and played most of his golf on the American Tour. Sutton went for Stewart Cink and Jay Haas, who had turned 50 that year, making him the second-oldest Ryder Cup player after Ray Floyd (who was 51 when he played in 1993).

At the opening ceremony, the two captains announced their playing orders for the next morning. When Sutton read out the first two names – Woods and Mickelson – the spectators went barmy.

But Europe won the opening fourballs 3½–½, giving the Americans a lesson in how to putt on the bumps and rolls of Oakland Hills' greens. Mongomerie and Harrington, who had been paired together in the second-day fourball matches at the Belfry, continued from where they left off. Playing Woods and Mickelson, Montgomerie hit his approach at the 1st to 7ft and holed the putt for a birdie to make it one up to Europe. By the 8th, the pair had collected five more birdies. It was left to Mickelson to rally on the back nine, and he kept himself and Woods in the match by holing out from 25ft at the 16th. Despite this, a par three at the next gave Europe the point. After beating Woods and Mickelson, Mongomerie commented, 'We feel, as a team, it was worth a little bit more than a point.'

Four birdies on the front nine saw Clarke and Jimenez go four up against Love III and

Campbell. Another birdie at the 11th then took them to five up, which they held on to until the 14th, where they completed a comfortable 5 and 4 win. Sergio Garcia and Lee Westwood claimed Europe's third point with a 5 and 3 victory over David Toms and Jim Furyk. The Americans narrowly avoided a morning whitewash thanks to Riley and Cink, who held on to square their match with McGinley and Donald.

Tiger Woods and Davis Love III can't bear to watch during their 4&3 defeat to Padraig Harrington and Paul McGinley in Saturday's foursomes.

In the afternoon foursomes, the United States team managed to win its first and only full point of the day when DiMarco and Haas beat Jimenez and Levet 3 and 2. But from there on in things just got better and better for the Europeans. Montgomerie and Harrington beat an out-of-form Davis Love III and debutant Fred Funk 4 and 2. Paired together again, Woods and Mickelson, ranked second and fourth in the world respectively, were starting to look like champions when they went three up in no time at all against Clarke and Westwood. But on the 10th hole the Europeans drew level. Clarke hit his approach to 4ft and

Westwood did the rest. At the next they took the lead, holding on to it at the 18th and leaving Hal Sutton to stare into the middle distance wondering what on earth was going on. When Luke Donald and Sergio Garcia beat Kenny Perry and Stewart Cink 2 and 1, Europe had creating history by recording their biggest opening day total in all the Ryder Cups. The score was an unbelievable 1½–6½.

Europe had profited from Sutton's misjudgement on the first day. The Woods and Mickelson pairing had not only failed, but had backfired on the American captain. Montgomerie and Harrington's win sent out a signal of strength to the rest of the European team.

The periscope is an essential bit of spectator kit at any Ryder Cup.

The second day would hinge on the last fourball match before lunch. The Americans had fought back strongly on the second morning and suddenly it was the Europeans who were missing the short putts. Haas and DiMarco set the tone in the first match, against Garcia and Westwood, by holing a 10ft birdie putt at the 1st. By the 6th the Americans had doubled the lead, but then back came Europe to level the match at the 11th. At the 18th Garcia holed an impossible putt for a five and secured a half. Meanwhile, behind them, Tiger Woods teamed up with Riley (his tenth partner in Ryder Cup matches) and comfortably won 4 and 3 against Poulter and Clarke.

With Montgomerie and Harrington losing their match, it was left to Casey and Howell to try to salvage something from the morning. Things looked good for Europe when Casey birdied the long 10th, but Furyk re-discovered his touch and holed three birdie putts on the trot to turn a two-hole deficit into a one-hole lead. Howell won the 17th to level the match and Casey completed the turn-around at the last to complete an unlikely and vital point for Europe. 'Our team was being hammered all morning,' said Howell. 'We feel like we've dodged a bullet.'

The momentum of the win in the last morning fourball carried Europe through the afternoon. Westwood and Clarke birdied the 1st and were four up after 11 on DiMarco and Haas. The victory was never in doubt and came at the 14th. Garcia and Donald, the two youngest members of the team, clung on to a slender lead against Furyk and Funk to win by one hole. And with Harrington and McGinley's win of 4 and 3, Europe had created more history by achieving their biggest ever lead going into the singles: the score was 11–5.

For a short time on Sunday afternoon, European nerves became frayed. Predictably, Sutton had sent out his best players first. Tiger Woods, Phil Mickelson, Davis Love III and Jim Furyk started the singles with an onslaught on Paul Casey, Sergio Garcia, Darren Clarke and David Howell. Briefly, the spectre of Brookline loomed ominously. But it was short-lived American pressure, and once Garcia (who was two down at the 8th) started holing putts to reel Mickelson in, eventually beating him at the 16th to win 3 and 2, it was the beginning of the end for the home team. A half for Clarke with Love III made it 12½ points to Europe. Woods did his job and beat Casey 3 and 2, and Furyk beat Howell 6 and 4, but the race was now on to see who could sink the winning putt.

It didn't take long to find out. Lee Westwood had taken Europe to the brink. Having led the charge on the final day at the Belfry in 2002, Colin

The victorious European team who recorded their biggest winning margin in the history of the competition.

Montgomerie would now have the honour of holing the putt to win the Cup. Playing David Toms, Montgomerie needed a par at the last to win. He left himself a nasty little 4ft putt, but in it went. Montgomerie dropped his putter and at the back of the green embraced his captain. It was a high point in what for him had been a very low year.

The singles successes kept coming for Europe, with Levet, Poulter, Harrington and McGinley taking the final total to 18½–9½, the biggest win in history by a European team. It was also the biggest margin of victory since the Americans dismantled Europe at Walton Heath in 1981. Some wag even suggested afterwards that the United States ought to think about expanding its selection process to include Canada and Mexico.

'I thought there was no bad way to pair our 12 guys,' Sutton said to reporters afterwards. 'Obviously the pairings we sent out didn't create any charisma.' His comments went a long way to explaining why the match had been so disastrous for the Americans. Langer, who at times seemed to be invisible as a captain, had, in fact, constantly been plotting his next move.

After winning his third US Open title at Oakland Hills in 1951, Ben Hogan had famously expressed his joy at having 'brought this course, this monster, to its knees'. In 2004 European professionals had brought the American Ryder Cup team to its knees. The victory was reminiscent of the master-class that the Americans had routinely handed out to British and European teams of the past.

From small seeds the Ryder Cup has grown into a global sporting event, attracting tens of millions of viewers worldwide. For both the journeymen and the superstars of golf, making a Ryder Cup team remains one of the highlights of their playing careers. 2006 is another landmark year for the Ryder Cup, as the competition is played on Irish soil for the first time. Europe and America will add a new drama to the script at the K Club in County Kildare. The outcome is as unpredictable as the game of golf itself.

2004 OAKLAND HILLS COUNTRY CLUB, BLOOMFIELD TOWNSHIP, MICHIGAN

EUROPE			UNITED STATES
— FOURBALLS — MORNING			
C. Montgomerie & P. Harrington (2 & 1)	1	0	P. Mickelson & T. Woods
D. Clarke & M.A. Jiménez (5 & 4)	1	0	D. Love III & C. Campbell
P. McGinley & L. Donald (halved)	½	½	C. Riley & S. Cink (halved)
S. Garcia & L. Westwood (5 & 3)	1	0	D. Toms & J. Furyk
— FOURSOMES — AFTERNOON			
M.A. Jimenez & T. Levet	0	1	C. DiMarco & J. Haas (3 & 2)
C. Montgomerie & P. Harrington (5 & 4)	1	0	J. Furyk & F. Funk
D. Clarke & L. Westwood (1 hole)	1	0	T. Woods & P. Mickelson
S. Garcia & L. Donald (2 & 1)	1	0	K. Perry & S. Cink
— FOURBALLS — MORNING			
S. Garcia & L. Westwood (halved)	½	½	J. Haas & C. DiMarco (halved)
D. Clarke & I. Poulter	0	1	T. Woods & C. Riley (4 & 3)
P. Casey & D. Howell (1 hole)	1	0	J. Furyk & C. Campbell
C. Montgomerie & P. Harrington	0	1	S. Cink & D. Love III (3 & 2)
— FOURSOMES — AFTERNOON			
D. Clarke & L. Westwood (5 & 4)	1	0	J. Haas & C. DiMarco
M.A. Jimenez & T. Levet	0	1	P. Mickelson & D. Toms (4 & 3)
S. Garcia & L. Donald (1 hole)	1	0	J. Furyk & F. Funk
P. Harrington & P. McGinley (4 & 3)	1	0	T. Woods & D. Love III
— SINGLES — SUNDAY			
P. Casey	0	1	T. Woods (3 & 2)
S. Garcia	1	0	P. Mickelson
D. Clarke (halved)	½	½	D. Love III (halved)
D. Howell	0	1	J. Furyk (6 & 4)
L. Westwood (1 hole)	1	0	K. Perry
C. Montgomerie (1 hole)	1	0	D. Toms
L. Donald	0	1	C. Campbell (5 & 3)
M.A. Jimenez	0	1	C. DiMarco (1 hole)
T. Levet (1 hole)	1	0	F. Funk
I. Poulter (3 & 2)	1	0	C. Riley
P. Harrington (1 hole)	1	0	J. Haas
P. McGinley (3 & 2)	1	0	S. Cink

VICTORIOUS CAPTAIN

BERNHARD LANGER

18½   **9½**

INDEX